The Science of Getting Rich Action Pack

The Essential Guide to Using The Science of Getting Rich

By

Wallace Wattles and Larry McLauchlin

This book is a work of non-fiction. Names and places have been changed to protect the privacy of all individuals. The events and situations are true.

ISBN: 1-4140-1492-9 (e-book)
ISBN: 1-4140-1493-7 (Paperback)

Library of Congress Control Number: 2003097415

This book is printed on acid free paper.

Printed in the United States of America
Bloomington, IN

1stBooks – rev. 10/20/03

The Science of Getting Rich book included within The Science of Getting Rich Action Pack was originally published in 1910. It was the standard of the time to write in the masculine gender only; should this book be written today there would changes to the wording. Please view the masculine terminology in a generic manner.

To contact the author of this book,
please email mailto:larry@ProsperitySecrets.com
or visit his websites at **http://www.ProsperitySecrets.com/**
or **http://www.Spiritual-e-books.com/.**

Dedication

This book is dedicated the authors
of the early 1900s for giving their
uncommon wisdom so freely to the world.
Most notably; Christian D. Larson, Wallace D. Wattles,
James Allen and Charles F. Haanel.

Visit www.ProsperitySecrets.com to see
the great books by these and
other early 1900s Authors

Table of Contents

Preface From the Publisher ix

How to Use The Science of Getting Rich Action Pack x

Preface From The Science of Getting Rich xi

Chapter One - The Right To Be Rich 1

Chapter One - Taking Action.. 10

Chapter One - Completed Example Of Using This Action Pack 18

Chapter Two - There Is A Science Of Getting Rich 27

Chapter Two - Taking Action... 30

Chapter Three - Is Opportunity Monopolized? 41

Chapter Three - Taking Action 44

Chapter Four - The First Principle Of the Science Of Getting Rich........... 53

Chapter Four - Taking Action.. 57

Chapter Five - Increasing Life 67

Chapter Five - Taking Action... 71

Chapter Six - How Riches Come To You.. 83

Chapter Six - Taking Action 87

Chapter Seven - Gratitude 97

Chapter Seven - Taking Action 100

Chapter Eight - Thinking In The Certain Way 117

Chapter Eight - Taking Action 120

Chapter Nine - How To Use The Will 131

Chapter Nine - Taking Action 135

Chapter Ten - Further Use Of The Will 145

Chapter Ten - Taking Action 149

Chapter Eleven - Acting In A Certain Way 159

Chapter Eleven - Taking Action 163

Chapter Twelve - Efficient Action 173

Chapter Twelve - Taking Action 176

Chapter Thirteen - Getting Into The Right Business 187

Chapter Thirteen - Taking Action 190

Chapter Fourteen - The Impression Of Increase 199

Chapter Fourteen - Taking Action 202

Chapter Fifteen - The Advancing Man 211

Chapter Fifteen - Taking Action 214

Chapter Sixteen - Some Cautions, And Concluding Observations. 223

Chapter Sixteen - Taking Action 226

Chapter Seventeen - Summary Of Science Of Getting Rich 235

Final Actions: 237

Proven, Time-Tested Secrets And Materials That Work........239

The Science of Getting Rich

Preface From the Publisher

There is a Science of Getting Rich, an exact science, like algebra and arithmetic. There are certain laws that govern the process of acquiring riches; once these laws are learned and obeyed by anyone. They will get rich with mathematical certainty.

Wallace D. Wattles

Wallace D. Wattles published this magnificent little book in 1910. A practical little manual outlining exactly how anyone with average intelligence who follows the steps, he puts forth here, will certainly get rich.

The practical method for achieving financial and personal success presented by him has stood the test of time. The method presented here has been used by countless thousands in obtaining freedom from insecurity - both financially and emotionally. Wallace D. Wattles has provided the "certain way" – a simple and complete method, in the Science of Getting Rich book which when followed with faith and understanding will guide you to riches.

You deserve to be rich:

Man's right to life means his right to have the free and unrestricted use of all the things which may be necessary to his fullest mental, spiritual, and physical unfoldment; or, in other words, his right to be rich.

I urge you to take this little book, study it, use it, act on it and day by day as you take efficient action as given in this book – you will most certainly get rich. The Science of Getting Rich Action Pack was designed to assist you in studying, using, acting and internalizing the Universal Laws given in The Science of Getting Rich book.

How to Use The Science of Getting Rich Action Pack

I know that a person can read, study and act on the principles given in *The Science of Getting Rich* and get rich...in fact that is how Wallace Wattles turned his own life around. And it has made a tremendous difference to my own life.

But I also know that many people have read *The Science of Getting Rich* and not changed their life and finances one iota. Unfortunately this has happened to the majority of readers.

Why didn't these people get rich? Because just reading this book will not make you rich any more than reading a book on how to swim will not make you a swimmer. It takes more that that!

Clearly what is needed is:

> ➤ the ability to recognize the principles (Universal Laws) given,
> ➤ then be able to relate the principles to your own life,
> ➤ fully internalize and expect that the principles will make your life better,
> ➤ and finally, applying the principles until they become a habit.

This guide – *The Science of Getting Rich Action Pack* – was designed, based on how the human mind works, to provide the necessary process to ensure that you are able to recognize, relate, internalize and apply the principles in your own life so that you act in the "Certain Way" that will certainly make you rich.

The Science of Getting Rich Action Pack was designed to assist you in getting rich but you may use the same process for achieving any other desire in your life. More health. More happiness. More satisfying relationships. More of everything.

Larry McLauchlin, Calgary Alberta Canada, 2003

Preface From The Science of Getting Rich Book

This book is pragmatical, not philosophical; a practical manual, not a treatise upon theories. It is intended for the men and women whose most pressing need is for money, who wish to get rich first, and philosophize afterward. It is for those who have so far, found neither the time, the means, not the opportunity to go deeply into the study of metaphysics, but want results and who are willing to take the conclusions of science as a basis for action, without going into all the processes by which those conclusions were reached.

It is expected that the reader will take the fundamental statements upon faith, just as he would take statements concerning a law of electrical action if they were promulgated by a Marconi or an Edison, and, taking the statements upon faith, that he will prove their truth by acting upon them without fear or hesitation. Every man or woman who does this will certainly get rich, for the science herein applied is an exact science and failure is impossible. For the benefit, however, of those who wish to investigate philosophical theories and so secure a logical basis for faith, I will here cite certain authorities.

The monistic theory of the universe – the theory that One is All, and that All is One; that one Substance manifests itself as the seeming many elements of the material world – is of Hindu origin, and has been gradually winning its way into the thought of western world for two hundred years. It is the foundation of all the Oriental philosophies, and those of Descartes, Spinoza, Leibnitz, Schopenhauer, Hegel and Emerson.

The reader who would dig to the philosophical foundations is advised to read Hegel and Emerson for himself.

In writing this book I have sacrificed all other considerations to plainness and simplicity of style, so that all might understand. The plan of action laid down herein was deduced from the conclusions of philosophy; it has been thoroughly tested, and bears the supreme test of practical experiment: It works. If you wish to know how the conclusions were arrived at, read the writings of the authors mentioned above;

and if you wish to reap the fruits of their philosophies in actual practice, read this book and do exactly as it tells you to do.

Wallace Wattles, 1910

Chapter One - The Right To Be Rich

Whatever may be said in praise of poverty, the fact remains that it is not possible to live a really complete or successful life unless one is rich. No man can rise to his greatest possible height in talent or soul development unless he has plenty of money; for to unfold the soul and to develop talent he must have many things to use, and he cannot have these things unless he has money with which to buy them.

Man develops in mind, soul, and body by making use of things, and society is so organized that man must have money in order to become the possessor of things; therefore, the basis of all advancement for man must be the science of getting rich.

The object of all life is development; and everything that lives has an alienable right to all the development it is capable of attaining.

Man's right to life means his right to have the free and unrestricted use of all the things which may be necessary to his fullest mental, spiritual, and physical unfoldment; or, in other words, his right to be rich.

In this book, I shall not speak of riches in a figurative way; to be really rich does not mean to be satisfied or contented with a little. No man ought to be satisfied with a little if he is capable of using and enjoying more. The purpose of Nature is the advancement and unfoldment of life; every man should have all that can contribute to the power, elegance, beauty, and richness of life; to be content with less is sinful.

The man who owns all he wants for the living of all the life he is capable of living is rich, and no man who has not plenty of money can have all he wants. Life has advanced so far, and become so complex, that even the most ordinary man or woman requires a great amount of wealth in order to live in a manner that even approaches completeness. Every person naturally wants to become all that he is capable of becoming; this desire to realize innate possibilities is inherent in human nature; we cannot help wanting to be all that we can be. Success in life is becoming what you want to be; you can become what you want to be only by making use of things, and you can have the free use of things only as you become

1

rich enough to buy them. To understand the science of getting rich is therefore the most essential of all knowledge.

There is nothing wrong in wanting to get rich. The desire for riches is really the desire for a richer, fuller, and more abundant life, and that desire is praiseworthy. The man who does not desire to live more abundantly is abnormal, and so the man who does not desire to have money enough to buy all he wants is abnormal.

There are three motives for which we live: we live for the body, we live for the mind, we live for the soul. No one of these is better or holier than the others; all are alike desirable, and no one of the three - body, mind or soul - can live fully if either of the others is cut short of full life and expression. It is not right or noble to live only for the soul and deny mind or body, and it is wrong to live for the intellect and deny body and soul.

We are all acquainted with the loathsome consequences of living for the body and denying both mind and soul; we see that real life means the complete expression of all that man can give forth through body, mind and soul. Whatever he may say, no man can be really happy or satisfied unless his body is living fully in every function, and unless the same is true of his mind and his soul. Wherever there is unexpressed possibility, or function not performed, there is unsatisfied desire. Desire is possibility seeking expression, or function seeking performance.

Man cannot live fully in body without good food, comfortable clothing and warm shelter, and without freedom from excessive toil. Rest and recreation are also necessary to his physical life.

He cannot live fully in mind without books and time to study them, without opportunity for travel and observation, or without intellectual companionship.

To live fully in mind he must have intellectual recreations, and must surround himself with all the objects of art and beauty he is capable of using and appreciating.

To live fully in soul, man must have love, and love is denied expression by poverty. .

Man's highest happiness is found in the bestowal of benefits on those he loves; love finds its most natural and spontaneous expression in giving. The man who has nothing to give cannot fill his place as a husband or father, as a citizen, or as a man. It is in the use of material things that man finds full life for his body, develops his mind, and unfolds his soul. It is therefore of supreme importance to him that he should be rich.

It is perfectly right that you should desire to be rich; if you are a normal man or woman you cannot help doing so. It is perfectly right that you should give your best attention to the Science of Getting Rich, for it is the noblest and most necessary of all studies. If you neglect this study, you are derelict in your duty to yourself, to God, and to humanity; for you can render God and humanity no greater service than to make the most of yourself.

My Commitment to Completing The Science of Getting Rich Course

I am starting The Science of Getting Rich Action Pack on __22/3__ , 20__66__

Monday 14 October 2013

My Commitment

☑ I commit to enthusiastically studying and digesting the material of The Science of Getting Rich Action Pack.

☑ I will use the information on faith and do what is asked of me.

☑ I commit to completing all the exercises and activities required in The Science of Getting Rich Action Pack.

☑ I commit to reading the Science of Getting Rich Book daily.

☑ I commit to making every effort required to completely <u>understand</u> the principles in The Science of Getting Rich Action Pack.

☑ I commit to <u>acting</u> on the principles that I learn in The Science of Getting Rich Action Pack.

I fully and completely commit to the above.

Riana M. Dark   _R Thorpe-Tracey_
Signature

__22/3/06__   Mon 14 Oct 2013
Date

I can do extraordinary things with no tools other than my own conviction.

Preparing for The Science of Getting Rich Action Pack

Before you begin The Science of Getting Rich Action Pack sit down with this sheet of paper. In the next 5 minutes write down as many of your beliefs about money and getting rich as you possibly can. Do not think about this too much. Just write. Start now!

Money is for spending. Getting rich is hard work. People who get rich spend a lot of time worrying about money. If I have money I'll have to buy a bigger home. If I have a fancy home people will be jealous. I won't fit in with wealthy people. Wealthy people are tight. Extravagance is immoral. My family will be jealous if I am rich. If I am not rich who will look after my parents when I am old? Who will look after me when I'm old. People look down on my home, my street because I am not wealthy. Money = success security, happiness, I have resources + savings. Wealth is generated through assets, stocks + shares. The stock market is evil. Money is for buying things to show off. Buying gifts + meals out is how to show love.

Examples of Limiting Beliefs About Money and Getting Rich

If I become wealthy then I'll have to make lots of changes in my life.

Being wealthy would mean people would treat me differently.

I don't have the ambition to do what it takes to get rich.

Being wealthy will make my friend treat me differently.

I stay where I am at because I like my life the way it is.

I can't become wealthy because it would take to much time and energy.

I can't become wealthy because I have a full time job working for someone else.

I can't manage my money well enough to get rich.

I should be satisfied with what I have.

I don't deserve to be rich.

I can't make more money than my parents.

Rich people take advantage of others to get wealthy.

Being rich means I can't be spiritual.

Rich people are bad people.

Money is the root of all evil.

Money is scarce.

I don't ever have enough money.

Making money is hard work and a struggle.

I barely have enough money to pay my bills let alone save any.

I'm afraid I'll become a bag lady – alone, poor, old and scared.

I work hard for my money and I'll never have anything to show for it.

If I have money – I spend it.

No matter what I do there is never enough money.

I'm not smart enough.

I never was good with money.

It takes money to make money.

Men make the money. Women are the caregivers.

I'm too young to get rich.

I'm too old to get rich.

What if my thoughts actually become my experience?

Reviewing your list of beliefs about money and getting rich; consider this thought, "If my thoughts become my reality; is this the reality that I want to create with respect to money and getting rich?

Identify Three Detrimental Beliefs – You Want To Change

Choose what you believe to be your three most detrimental beliefs - beliefs that stop you from getting the money that you deserve. Take each belief and rewrite it in the opposite or positive manner. Write them on a 3 x 5 card. Read and contemplate them morning and evening for the next seven days.

Example of negative beliefs:

1. I never was good with money.
2. It takes money to make money.
3. There is only so much money in the world – if I get rich I will be taking money from someone else.

Example of re-written beliefs:

1. I am able to learn to manage my money.
2. I can start right where I am and learn the how to get rich.
3. The world is abundant; there is no scarcity

"As you continue to read and study The Science of Getting Rich book and work thought The Science of Getting Rich Action Pack. You will find yourself easily and naturally making changes to your limited money beliefs"

The Key to Using the Principles in The Science of Getting Rich Book…
To Get Rich

Recognize, Relate, Assimilate And Apply The Principles In This Course

Why is it that some people can read a book and it changes their life for the better right away while others can read the same book and nothing happens? Somehow some people are able to take the important principles from the book and automatically put them to work in their life. They get results immediately. Others need a formula, process or system to achieve the same results.

We have incorporated a formula or process that will assist you in recognizing the principles or laws in each chapter of The Science of Getting Rich and relate them to your own life, assimilate them - understand them and apply them daily in your life for improved results.

Your ability to recognize, relate, assimilate and apply this formula to the principles in the Science of Getting Rich book can lead you to wealth, success and happiness. The Science of Getting Rich provides fundamental principles which when followed will certainly cause you to get rich. A principle is a basic truth – a universal law that does not change.

Recognize - is to identify the principle, idea or technique.

Relate - is to connect or join together, to establish a relationship to you own life.

Assimilate - is to incorporate, to absorb, to become part of.

Apply - is to use, to act upon, to do.

The Recognize, Relate, Assimilate and Apply Formula should become so ingrained in your mind that you can RECOGNIZE wealth principles from books, lectures, newspapers, bibliographies, and many other sources. It should become a mental reflex.

The "**Putting the Science of Getting Rich Principles to Work**" form, an example of this form is shown on the next page, will help you easily take ideas, concepts, and Universal Laws that you will discover using this course from the abstract to something concrete that you can use and internalize in your own life.

Two examples of how to use the, "**Putting the Science of Getting Rich Principles to Work"** form, and the recognize, relate, assimilate and apply principles are given in Chapter One of this course.

Putting the Science of Getting Rich Principles to Work

Recognize: Principle One I recognize in this Chapter is:

I have the right to be rich

Relate: What does this mean to me? What will this principle do for me?

I deserve the wealth + abundance and my limiting beliefs are all that is stopping me.

Assimilate: How can I use the principles to achieve my goals/riches?

I can turn my limiting beliefs into positive ones

Apply: How am I going to use it? Action steps. Do It Now!

I am going to contemplate my positive beliefs each morning + night + integrate them into my very being.

Chapter One - Taking Action
Understanding Chapter One
The Right to Be Rich

1.   Why should all persons make the Science of Getting Rich a priority for their life?

We live in a world governed by money so in order to grow spiritually, materially we need resources to do this. We need it to live a full + complete life.

2.   Why are riches necessary for one to live a complete life?

We need to have the resources + the things to balance the mind, body + soul. You cannot rise to your full potential without riches.

3.   What is the purpose of Nature?

To grow + expand continously. The advancement + unfoldment of life

4.   Explain why it is important to have a balance in the three motives for which we live: body, mind and soul?

All are equally important + neither is better or more worthy than the other

5.   How do riches help a person develop in body, mind and soul?

It is best to fully express each aspect + again we need riches to express love, to have comfort + to stimulate the mind.

6.   What is your personal balance of mind, body and spirit?

I spend money + time on books + courses ~~+ doing~~ on spirit + ~~for~~ doing spiritual work. I would like to spend more time + resources on my body - exercise + good food. My knowledge/mind is more on spirit but I want to learn more about finances.

7.   Are their changes you need to make to this balance? If yes, what will you do to make the changes? When?

Yes I will change now my diet - buying more food to cook at home + eating out less. I will go to hot yoga more often + get to bed earlier, keep warm + active + eat better.

"We must manifest things, and it is not wrong to do so, because matter is the necessary channel for the self-differentiation of Spirit."

"We are what we assume ourselves to be; and may be what we determine to be."

"I know this much for sure – there is one power, one Intelligence, one Formless Substance that permeates every atom of matter and every unit of energy and all space. This formless Substance may through the principles in the Science of Getting Rich be used in the aid of transmuting desires into concrete material form."

"Commit to proceeding…even thought you might be on the fringe of fear."

"You have complete responsibility for your success, your future and for what you do with this valuable knowledge."

Chapter One Learnings

The most important principles, concepts and thoughts that I have learned from this Chapter are:

1. My beliefs about money + making money are limiting my ability to make money ✓

2. Money + making money can be taught + learnt ✓

3. The world is abundant + their is no scarcity. ✓

4. It is my right to have Money in order to live a fulfilling, balanced life ✓

5. It's up to me to make these changes in my life to have abundance, resources + RICHES ✓

6. A balance of mind, body + spirit is only really possible with RICHES

7. I can start learning how to obtain riches right here + now from where I am now. ✓

8. The purpose of Nature is to grow constantly + expand + prosper!

Chapter One Learnings

The two most Important principles, concepts and thoughts that I have learned from this Chapter and will use in my life are:

Principle One:

It is my divine right, my duty to continously grow + expand, to generate wealth + prosperity, to ~~have to~~ fulfill my best potential.

Principle Two:

I do not have to wait to be abundant. The balance of mind, body + Spirit + ~~the~~ continous growth ~~of the~~ Nature Success means becoming what I can and want to be. I can only do this with resources + riches

"When riches begin to come they come so quickly, in such great abundance that one wonders where they have been hiding during all those years." – Napoleon Hill.

Putting the Science of Getting Rich Principles to Work

Recognize: Principle One I recognize in this Chapter is:

It is my duty to be rich

Relate: What does this mean to me? What will this principle do for me?

I must reach my full potential.
In order to do this, I must organise my finances,
now. I must set plans for saving for my future,
for my work, for getting mortgage-free
+ for changing my attitude to money.
What is it I really desire

Assimilate: How can I use the principles to achieve my goals/riches?

I will seek advice on the best ways to
make money from people I trust — not
just for my future but for my family.
I will find out what I want +
concentrate on this.

Apply: How am I going to use it? Action steps. Do It Now!

I am going to start over-paying on my mortgage.
I will work out where my spending is going
+ ~~where~~ how much money I have coming in
+ how much I have saved in my pensions.
I can work out how much I have
coming in + going out + take action
accordingly i.e. cut down on eating out.
I am going to create a rich + full
wish book of all the things I desire TOMORROW
MORNING

Putting the Science of Getting Rich Principles to Work

Recognize: Principle Two I recognize in this Chapter is:

It's important to live in balance
with mind, body + soul.
Success means BECOMING MY FULL POTENTIAL
+ I need resources + money to get those
things.

Relate: What does this mean to me? What will this principle do for me?

I need to spend time on working
on my needs as to have
eating well + execercising
+ using my resources to have
a balance. Material things are absolutely
necessary to achieve a fulfilling life.

Assimilate: How can I use the principles to achieve my goals/riches?

Making sure I have enough time
to rest + relax, to exercise,
to have fun, to innovate
to be better at managing
finances. I will replace my beliefs with
a knowledge for learning about I deserve
abundance

Apply: How am I going to use it? Action steps. Do It Now!

Use Sri AmmaBhagavan! Pray!
Do the exercises in this book
Make a wish book
Do my online OMS
Sort out my monthly spending
Start overpaying my mortgage
Start sharedealing
Start paying into pensions.

As a result of your new learnings list the actions or goals will you are going to accomplish, so that you too can become rich by doing things "in a certain way"

1. Start planning what I really want from life

2. Finding out all I can about share-dealing

3. Making sure I educate myself about Money

4. Learning not to listen to people's limiting beliefs

5. Changing my limiting beliefs

6. Being brave + getting help about Money.

Chapter One - Completed Example Of Using This Action Pack

Success Process for maximum benefit.

For

Chapter One

The Right to Be Rich

The Science of Getting Rich
Understanding Chapter One
The Right to Be Rich

1.   Why should all persons make the Science of Getting Rich a priority for their life?

No man or woman can live a complete life unless they have plenty of money; for to unfold the soul and develop their talent they must have plenty of things to use – and they cannot have these things unless they have money to purchase them. Even Mother Teresa could not have helped the poor if she had not have access to money.

2.   Why are riches necessary for one to live a complete life?

People develop in mind, soul and body by making use of things, and society is organized that we must have money to possess these things – therefore the bases of all advancement is the science of getting rich.

3.   What is the purpose of Nature?

The purpose of Nature is the advancement and the unfoldment of life. Everyone should have all that can contribute to the power, elegance, beauty, and richness of life. To be content with less it to live a less than complete life.

4.   Explain why it is important to have a balance in the three motives for which we live: body, mind and soul?

There are 3 motives for which we live – body, mind and soul. No one motive is better or holier than the other – all are alike desirable. No one of these motives can be fully expressed without fully living and developing the other two.

5.   How do riches help a person develop in body, mind and soul?

We cannot live fully in body without good food, comfortable clothing, warm shelter, rest, recreation and freedom from excess toil. We cannot live fully in mind without books and time to study the,

the opportunity to travel and observe, or without intellectual companionship. We cannot live fully in soul without love and love is denied expression by poverty.

6.   What is your personal balance of mind, body and spirit?

I am out of balance. I have concentrated more on mind and spirit. If I were to estimate this balance if would be – mind - 40%; body – 20% and spirit or soul – 40%

7.   Are their changes you need to make to this balance? If yes, what will you do to make the changes? When?

Yes, changes are required. I need to pay more attention to "body."

Begin an exercise program – walk for half hour, five times a week – starting April 15, 2002. Eat per the low carbohydrate eating plan – start tonight at supper.

Chapter One Learnings

The most Important principles, concepts and thoughts that I have learned from this Chapter are:

1. It is not possible for me to live a really complete or successful life unless one is prosperous.

2. My right to life means my right to have a free and unrestricted use of all the things that are necessary for my fullest, mental, spiritual and physical unfoldment.

3. I need not be satisfied with little when I am capable of using and enjoying more.

4. Success in life means becoming what I can and want to be. I can only become what I want to be by making the free use of things and I can only have the free use of things if I have plenty of money to purchase those things.

5. The desire for riches is really the desire for a richer, fuller and more abundant life. That desire is praiseworthy.

6. I live for the body, mind and soul. No one of these motives is better than the other. There must be balance – to live a balanced life.

7. The use of material things allows me to find full life for my body, develop my mind and unfold my soul. It is therefore of extreme importance to study and apply the science of getting rich.

8. It is perfectly natural and right that I have a strong desire to get rich.

Chapter One Learnings

The two most Important principles, concepts and thoughts that I have learned from this Chapter and will use in my life are:

Principle One:

It is not possible for me to live a really complete or successful life unless one is prosperous.

Principle Two:

Success in life means becoming what I can and want to be. I can only become what I want to be by making the free use of things and I can only have the free use of things if I have plenty of money to purchase those things.

Putting the Science of Getting Rich Principles to Work

Recognize: Principle One I recognize in this Chapter is:

It is not possible for me to live a really complete or successful life unless one is prosperous.

Relate: What does this mean to me? What will this principle do for me?

It means that if I really want to live a full, complete, successful, and happy life, I need to determine what it is that will make me feel complete, successful and happy. What is it that I really desire?

Assimilate: How can I use the principles to achieve my goals/riches?

I will begin to think about what it is that I want and replace all thoughts about what it is that I do not want.

Apply: How am I going to use it? I will take these action steps. Do It Now!

I will set aside four hours this weekend to spend some time alone determining what it is that I truly desire. I will put these thoughts in writing. I will review and update my desire daily by the use of a goal card. I will follow the principles set out in this course to achieve my desires.

Putting the Science of Getting Rich Principles to Work

Recognize: Principle Two I recognize in this Chapter is:

Success in life means becoming what I can and want to be. I can only become what I want to be by making the free use of things and I can only have the free use of things if I have plenty of money to purchase those things.

Relate: What does this mean to me? What will this principle do for me?

I now know that material things are not only useful but they are absolutely necessary to live a full and complete life.

Assimilate: How can I use the principles to achieve my goals/riches?

I will replace the belief that being rich and having things is not spiritual.

Apply: How am I going to use it? I will take these action steps. Do It Now!

I will read Chapter One twice a day for one week.

I will use the following affirmation daily. "It is through the use of material things that I live a full and complete life - to develop my mind, unfold my soul and perfect by body."

As a result of your new learnings list the actions or goals will you are going to accomplish, so that you too can become rich by doing things "in a certain way"

1.   Determine what I really want. In these areas: mind, body, soul development, career, family and social life.

2.   Write down these desires. Which of these desires are the strongest. Start with this desire – how will I achieve it?

3.   Immediately replace all thoughts about "A rich man cannot enter Heaven."

4.   Put my energy into getting what I want and stop putting my energy into what I do not what.

5.   Use the Recognize, Relate, Assimilate and Apply process on the two principles that I have chosen from this Chapter.

6.   Read this chapter twice a day this week.

Chapter Two - There Is A Science Of Getting Rich

There is a Science of Getting Rich, and it is an exact science, like algebra or arithmetic. There are certain laws which govern the process of acquiring riches; once these laws are learned and obeyed by any man, he will get rich with mathematical certainty.

The ownership of money and property comes as a result of doing things in a certain way; those who do things in this Certain Way, whether on purpose or accidentally, get rich; while those who do not do things in this Certain Way, no matter how hard they work or how able they are, remain poor.

It is a natural law that like causes always produce like effects; therefore, any man or woman who learns to do things in this Certain Way will infallibly get rich.

That the above statement is true is shown by the following facts:

Getting rich is not a matter of environment, for if it were, all the people in certain neighborhoods would become wealthy; the people of one city would all be rich, while those of other towns would all be poor; or the inhabitants of one state would roll in wealth, while those of an adjoining state would be in poverty.

But everywhere we see rich and poor living side by side, in the same environment, and often engaged in the same vocations. When two men are in the same locality, and in the same business, and one gets rich while the other remains poor, it shows that getting rich is not, primarily, a matter of environment. Some environments may be more favorable than others, but when two men in the same business are in the same neighborhood, and one gets rich while the other fails, it indicates that getting rich is the result of doing things in a Certain Way.

And further, the ability to do things in this Certain Way is not due solely to the possession of talent, for many people who have great talent remain poor, while others who have very little talent get rich.

Studying the people who have got rich, we find that they are an average lot in all respects, having no greater talents and abilities than other men. It is evident that they do not get rich because they possess talents and abilities that other men have not, but because they happen to do things in a Certain Way.

Getting rich is not the result of saving, or "thrift"; many very penurious people are poor, while free spenders often get rich.

Nor is getting rich due to doing things which others fail to do; for two men in the same business often do almost exactly the same things, and one gets rich while the other remains poor or becomes a bankrupt.

From all these things, we must come to the conclusion that getting rich is the result of doing things in a Certain Way.

If getting rich is the result of doing things in a Certain Way, and if like causes always produce like effects, then any man or woman who can do things in that way can become rich, and the whole matter is brought within the domain of exact science.

The question arises here, whether this Certain Way may not be so difficult that only a few may follow it. This cannot be true, as we have seen, so far as natural ability is concerned. Talented people get rich, and blockheads get rich; intellectually brilliant people get rich, and very stupid people get rich; physically strong people get rich, and weak and sickly people get rich.

Some degree of ability to think and understand is, of course, essential; but insofar as natural ability is concerned, any man or woman who has sense enough to read and understand these words can certainly get rich.

Also, we have seen that it is not a matter of environment. Location counts for something; one would not go to the heart of the Sahara and expect to do successful business.

Getting rich involves the necessity of dealing with men, and of being where there are people to deal with; if these people are inclined to deal in the way you want to deal, so much the better. But that is about as far as environment goes.

If anybody else in your town can get rich, so can you; and if anybody else in your state can get rich, so can you.

Again, it is not a matter of choosing some particular business or profession. People get rich in every business, and in every profession; while their next door neighbors in the same vocation remain in poverty.

It is true that you will do best in a business which you like, and which is congenial to you; if you have certain talents which are well developed, you will do best in a business which calls for the exercise of those talents.

Also, you will do best in a business which is suited to your locality; an ice cream parlor would do better in a warm climate than in Greenland, and a salmon fishery will succeed better in the Northwest than in Florida, where there are no salmon.

Aside from these general limitations, getting rich is not dependent upon your engaging in some particular business, but upon your learning to do things in a Certain Way. If you are now in business, and anybody else in your locality is getting rich in the same business, while you are *not* getting rich, it is because you are not doing things in the same Way that the other person is doing them.

No one is prevented from getting rich by lack of capital. True, as you get capital the increase becomes more easy and rapid; but one who has capital is already rich, and does not need to consider how to become so. No matter how poor you may be, if you begin to do things in the Certain Way you will begin to get rich, and you will be begin to have capital. The getting of capital is a part of the process of getting rich, and it is a part of the result which invariably follows the Certain Way.

You may be the poorest man on the continent, and be deeply in debt; you may have neither friends, influence or resources; but if you begin to do things in this Way; you must infallibly begin to get rich, for like causes must produce like effects. If you have no capital, you can get capital; if you are in the wrong business, you can get into the right business; if you are in the wrong location, you can go to the right location; you can do so by *beginning in your present business and in your present location* to do things in the Certain Way which causes success.

Chapter Two - Taking Action
Understanding Chapter Two
There is a Science of Getting Rich

1. Why does Wattles say there is a science of getting rich?

    There are certain laws that govern the universe + if we work with these laws (a certain way) we can get rich.

2. Describe why environment cannot be the cause of riches.

    Everywhere we see rich + poor living side by side -

3. Describe why talent cannot be the cause of riches.

    We see people without talent becoming rich

4. Describe why savings and thrift cannot be the cause of riches.

    Many spenders are rich Many thrifty people remain poor

5. Describe why doing things that others fail to do cannot be the cause of riches.

    Two people in the same business often do the same things but one becomes rich + the other remains poor.

6.   Describe why being in a particular industry or profession cannot be the cause of riches.

People in every industry get rich while the same, others in the same industry remain poor.

7.   Describe why lack of capital cannot be the cause of riches.

Getting Capital is the process of getting rich.

"There is no surer way along the "Pathway to Financial Success" than to follow in the footsteps of those who have reached it – begin now to act in that 'Certain Way.'"

"Everything on the world is made of energy. It is as easy to pour this energy into a mould of riches as it is to pour it into a mould of lack and poverty."

"See it Big; Keep it Simple."

Chapter Two Learnings

The most Important principles, concepts and thoughts that I have learned from this Chapter are:

1. Getting rich is an exact science

2. By following a certain way I can get rich

3. It is a natural law to getting rich

4. Environment is irrelevant to getting rich

5. Talent has nothing to do with getting rich

6. Saving or thrift has nothing to do
    with being getting rich

7. It's better to do a g profession that
    you enjoy

8. Capital is no barrier to getting rich
    it's part of the process.

Chapter One Learnings

The two most Important principles, concepts and thoughts that I have learned from this Chapter and will use in my life are:

Principle One:

There is an exact science to getting rich. It's a natural law and open to anyone.

Principle Two:

There are no barriers to me using these principles:
- enviroment
- thrift
- profersion
- capital
- talent

"Success comes to those who become success conscious.
Failure comes to those who in difficulty allow themselves to become failure conscious."
- Napoleon Hill.

Putting the Science of Getting Rich Principles to Work

Recognize: Principle One I recognize in this Chapter is:

There is an exact Science to getting rich

Relate: What does this mean to me? What will this principle do for me?

I can use a Certain way + Commit to generating my own wealth in order to

Assimilate: How can I use the principles to achieve my goals/riches?

I can learn the principles by reading learning + applying this law

Apply: How am I going to use it? Action steps. Do It Now!

I'm going to make a wish book!
I'm going to use all my resources to help me generate wealth.
I'm going to read this chapter + learn the exercises now.

Putting the Science of Getting Rich Principles to Work

Recognize: Principle Two I recognize in this Chapter is:

There are no barriers to me learning
how to get rich.

Relate: What does this mean to me? What will this principle do for me?

The way is open to me to be
rich. There is nothing stopping me.

Assimilate: How can I use the principles to achieve my goals/riches?

I can stop comparing myself to others
in age, talent, business sense,
industry, contacts, marketing.

Apply: How am I going to use it? Action steps. Do It Now!

I can create a wish book
+ work out all the things
I want + start learning
The science of getting rich.

A Clear and Definite Statement of My Desire

Write a clear and definite statement of your desire. What will you see, hear and feel when you have your desire. Make it sensory specific. Put emotion into your statement and end with an expression of gratitude.

Dear Bank Manager Sri Amma Bhagavan, Financial Advisor. Please help me to be completely debt-free, please help me to pay off the mortgage on 25 Viaduct Road within 2 years. Help me to set-up + manage well regular savings + help me to generate an income of at least £5555 per month. Please help me to have a warm + stylish home, in a safe calm area, with a seaview + countryside, to Please help me set up a wonderful welcoming centre: The Open Heart Oneness Centre - with a café and a venue + treatment rooms + space for courses + workshops. Help me to have 1000's of clients + generate an income of at least £555,000 each year. Help me to always have a fantastic reputation with loyal, devoted, trust worthy suppliers, staff, customers, clients, peers friends, and may everything I do be for the highest integrity + the best quality + a great success!

Treasure Map Your Way to Riches

A Treasure Map is a powerful way to create a tangible visualization of your desired riches.

Your Treasure Map will help you keep your focus and hold your desired riches in your mind.

A Treasure Map is a visual tool for building an inner experience of your desired result and thought that you wish to impress upon the One Source.

There are many ways to make Treasure Maps. You may draw, design or make a collage with cutouts from magazines. Choose paper, colors, ink, patterns, photos, pictures, phrases, and affirmations etc. that have special meaning to you. Make it as small or as big as you want.

You might consider doing both – making one small enough to carry with you each day and a larger one you can see often but others cannot. You may find it more dynamic if you place a picture of your self in your Treasure Maps.

When making your Treasure Map consider only what you want – do not place any limitations on it; whether it is too large a request or how it is to come about. These things are not your concerns; the Creative Power will bring you what ever you ask for in whatever ways It chooses to manifest it.

We are using a Treasure Map here to bring you riches. The same process can be used for relationships, characteristics, emotional well being or spiritual goals.

You might also decide to include an affirmation of gratitude such as, "I truly am grateful and I allow Formless Substance to manifest this or something better in my life."

When you have completed the Treasure Map, place it where you can see it everyday. Spend a few minutes each day looking at it and expressing your gratitude that you have already received it.

Keep your Treasure Map a secret.

Have faith that the One Source will provide you with everything you desire. In fact, you may want to include something in your Treasure Map that reminds you of your connection with the One Source.

Turn to the next page and complete your Treasure Map.

My Treasure Map

♡ I AM TRULY GRATEFUL TO THE DIVINE FOR MANIFESTING ALL OF THESE THINGS OR EVEN BETTER INTO MY LIFE. THANK YOU SRI AMMA BHAGAVAN, JESUS CHRIST † THE HOLY SPIRIT. ♡

TRAVEL all over the world
Swim with dolphins, surfing, scuba-diving, experiences, meeting famous + high quality people + becoming their friends

THE OPEN HEART
A venue, a space that generates at least £555,000 per annum, with fab reputation, a café a space for groups, co-working, workshops, treatments

RIFA THORPE TRACEY

A HAPPY HOME LIFE CALM + LOVING RELATIONSHIPS

A passive income of £5555 per month

well managed savings + investments

Mortgage paid off £100,000

a new home with a quiet country-side + a seaview

A really good studio set-up to do oneness meditations online

A popular radio show with a fantastic listenership sponsors + reputation

a fantastic reputation for good excellent quality work + the best clients customers suppliers staff friends

LOYALTY
INTEGRITY
QUALITY
LOVED BY ALL

Time to give healing, courses + write books articles + raise my profile to global status

Time to travel all over the country + the world doing God's work all paid for + generate an income too

39

As a result of your new learnings list the actions or goals will you are going to accomplish, so that you too can become rich by doing things "in a certain way"

1. Learn about share-dealing

2. Fill in Martin's budget tracker

3. Start putting more into mortgage

4. Get Chris to contribute £250 per month + past

5. Get Chris's £600 paid into the mortgage

6. Make ~~getting rid of~~ paying off the mortage a priority

Chapter Three - Is Opportunity Monopolized?

No man is kept poor because opportunity has been taken away from him, because other people have monopolized the wealth, and have put a fence around it. You may be shut off from engaging in business in certain lines, but there are other channels open to you. Probably it would be hard for you to get control of any of the great railroad systems; that field is pretty well monopolized. But the electric railway business is still in its infancy, and offers plenty of scope for enterprise; it will be but a very few years until traffic and transportation through the air will become a great industry, and in all its branches will give employment to hundreds of thousands, and perhaps to millions, of people. Why not turn your attention to the development of aerial transportation, instead of competing with J. J. Hill and others for a chance in the steam railway world?

It is quite true that if you are a workman in the employ of the steel trust you have very little chance of becoming the owner of the plant in which you work, but it is also true that if you will commence to act in a Certain Way, you can soon leave the employ of the steel trust; you can buy a farm of from ten to forty acres, and engage in business as a producer of foodstuffs. There is great opportunity at this time for men who will live upon small tracts of land and cultivate the same intensively; such men will certainly get rich. You may say that it is impossible for you to get the land, but I am going to prove to you that it is not impossible, and that you can certainly get a farm if you will go to work in a Certain Way.

At different periods the tide of opportunity sets in different directions, according to the needs of the Whole, and the particular stage of social evolution which has been reached. At present, in America, it is setting toward agriculture and the allied industries and professions. Today, opportunity is open before the farmer in his line more than before the factory worker in his line. It is open before the businessman who supplies the farmer more than before the one who supplies the factory worker, and before the professional man who waits upon the farmer more than before the one who serves the working class.

There is abundance of opportunity for the man who will go with the tide, instead of trying to swim against it.

So the factory workers, either as individuals or as a class, are not deprived of opportunity. The workers are not being "kept down" by their masters; they are not being "ground" by the trusts and combinations of capital. As a class, they are where they are because they do not do things in a Certain Way. If the workers of America chose to do so, they could follow the example of their brothers in Belgium and other countries, and establish great department stores and cooperative industries; they could elect men of their own class to office, and pass laws favoring the development of such cooperative industries; in a few years they could take peaceable possession of the industrial field.

The working class may become the master class whenever they will begin to do things in a Certain Way; the law of wealth is the same for them as it is for all others. This they must learn; and they will remain where they are as long as they continue to do as they do. The individual worker, however, is not held down by the ignorance or the mental slothfulness of his class; he can follow the tide of opportunity to riches, and this book will tell him how.

No one is kept in poverty by a shortness in the supply of riches; there is more than enough for all. A palace as large as the capitol at Washington might be built for every family on earth from the building material in the United States alone; under intensive cultivation, this country would produce wool, cotton, linen, and silk enough to clothe each person in the world finer than Solomon was arrayed in all his glory, together with food enough to feed them all luxuriously. The visible supply is *practically* inexhaustible, and the invisible supply really is inexhaustible.

Everything you see on earth is made from one original substance, out of which all things proceed.

New forms are constantly being made, and older ones are dissolving, but all are shapes assumed by One Thing.

There is no limit to the supply of Formless Stuff, or Original Substance. The universe is made out of it, but it was not all used in making the universe. The spaces in, through, and between the forms of the visible universe are permeated and filled with the Original Substance; with the Formless Stuff; with the raw material of all things. Ten thousand times as much as has been made might still be made, and even then we should not have exhausted the supply of universal raw material.

No man, therefore, is poor because nature is poor, or because there is not enough to go around.

Nature is an inexhaustible storehouse of riches; the supply will never run short. Original Substance is alive with creative energy, and is constantly producing more forms. When the supply of building material is exhausted, more will be produced; when the soil is exhausted so that foodstuffs and materials for clothing will no longer grow upon it, it will be renewed or more soil will be made. When all the gold and silver has been dug from the earth, if man is still in such a stage of social development that he needs gold and silver, more will be produced from the Formless. The Formless Stuff responds to the needs of man; it will not let him be without any good thing.

This is true of man collectively; the race as a whole is always abundantly rich, and if individuals are poor, it is because they do not follow the Certain Way of doing things which makes the individual man rich.

The Formless Stuff is intelligent; it is stuff which thinks. It is alive, and is always impelled toward more life.

It is the natural and inherent impulse of life to seek to live more; it is the nature of intelligence to enlarge itself, and of consciousness to seek to extend its boundaries and find fuller expression. The universe of forms has been made by Formless Living Substance, throwing itself into form in order to express itself more fully.

The universe is a great Living Presence, always moving inherently toward more life and fuller functioning.

Nature is formed for the advancement of life; its impelling motive is the increase of life. For this cause, everything which can possibly minister to life is bountifully provided; there can be no lack unless God is to contradict himself and nullify his own works.

You are not kept poor by lack in the supply of riches; it is a fact which I shall demonstrate a little farther on that even the resources of the Formless Supply are at the command of the man or woman who will act and think in a Certain Way.

Chapter Three - Taking Action
Understanding Chapter Three
Is Opportunity Monopolized

1. Why is opportunity not monopolized?

   There is always opportunities in new + expanding areas

2. How may anyone begin to take advantage of the Law of Wealth?

   We can all learn to do things in a certain way in order get riches!

3. Why is there no limit to Formless Stuff or Original Substance?

   The Universe is made of it but there is an inexhaustible supply of it!

4. Explain: "Nature is formed for the advancement of life."

   The whole world is made from Creative Energy that can never run out, it grows, changes, adapts, grows some more.

"Think BIG THOUGHTS – the Creative Energies of mind find no more difficulty in handling large situations than small ones. Mind is just as much present in the infinitely large as in the infinitely small."

Chapter Three Learnings

The most Important principles, concepts and thoughts that I have learned from this Chapter are:

1. _Opportunity is not limited to anyone_

2. _Anyone can learn to take advantage_
   by learning to do things in a
   certain way

3. _Everything you see on Earth is made_
   from one original Source

4. _There is no limit to this Source_
   No limit of resources, Crea

5. The Formless Stuff is intelligent
   + alive!

6. Working clan can rise up + be the
   Master clan

7. No-one is ~~keep~~ kept in poverty
   through lack of riches

8. No one is poor because the earth
   is ~~not~~ not poor.

Chapter Three Learnings

The two most Important principles, concepts and thoughts that I have learned from this Chapter and will use in my life are:

Principle One:

There are always opportunities to make
money

Principle Two:

The whole universe is made from an
inexhaustible abundant supply'

"We are surrounded by possibilities that can never be measured; possibilities which if employed even to a limited degree would make life many times as rich and beautiful as it is now." – Christian D. Larson.

"If you believe it will work out – you'll see opportunities."
If you believe that it will not work out – you'll see obstacles."
- Wayne Dyer

Putting the Science of Getting Rich Principles to Work

Recognize: Principle One I recognize in this Chapter is:

There are always opportunities

Relate: What does this mean to me? What will this principle do for me?

I have so many talents + skills. There is no limit to all the fun projects + things I can do + I can make money + keep money + grow money easily.

Assimilate: How can I use the principles to achieve my goals/riches?

I can keep adding to my wish list of fun ~~ways to make me to do~~ things to do + ~~ways to make~~ naturally money will come.

Apply: How am I going to use it? Action steps. Do It Now!

Make a list of all the fun things I want to do + follow up on the Radio Station thing + be more cheerful + have fun + take opportunities when they come!

Putting the Science of Getting Rich Principles to Work

Recognize: Principle Two I recognize in this Chapter is:

The Universe is abundant!

Relate: What does this mean to me? What will this principle do for me?

I cannot + will not limit myself or others!
I can write books, have a radio show,
run an event space + make so much
money in all different ways effortlessly
with style + grace

Assimilate: How can I use the principles to achieve my goals/riches?

I will not entertain any naysayers
I will to enjoy learning about money
+ being generous + careful with
spending but enjoying life.

Apply: How am I going to use it? Action steps. Do It Now!

I will ask for more every day
£ 100   £10,000
£ 100,000
£ 10,0,0000
are all available to me!
It is totally within my ability to earn
£555 per day + clear my mortgage.
within 2 years.

My Opportunity List

If I knew I could not fail I would _buy a property + turn it into The Open Heart cafe, event space, and meditation centre. + 'co-working'_

If I knew I could not fail I would _Swim with dolphins, travel the world (USA, Russia, South East Asia, Brazil Australia, New Zealand) exploring + loving the world._

If I knew I could not fail I would _set up my own media empire: books, magazines, website, broadcasts, podcasts, radio show, TV show, events, et c et._

"No man is kept poor because opportunity has been taken away from him, because other people have monopolized the wealth, and have put a fence around it."

You need not fail. You can achieve every one of these desires. The Science of Getting Rich shows you exactly what you are required to do to achieve your every desire. Decide exactly what you want and begin using the Science of Getting Rich principles to achieve it.

Here Are Several Ways That I Can Create Extra Income!

1. Bigger events that I charge for

2. Learn to trade online

3. Selling books + clothes I no longer want

4. Raising my consultancy fee

5. Doing a radio show + getting paid

6. Applying for funding

As a result of your new learnings list the actions or goals will you are going to accomplish, so that you too can become rich by doing things "in a certain way"

1. Learn to trade online

2. Make sure I know where my spending goes per month. – PER DAY!

3. Start po over-paying on mortgage

4. Raise the PM fee Get a job!?

5. Start planning a paid-for event

6. Start & looking for a co-working/ event/cafe centre space.

Chapter Four - The First Principle Of the Science Of Getting Rich

Thought is the only power which can produce tangible riches from the Formless Substance. The stuff from which all things are made is a substance which thinks, and a thought of form in this substance produces the form.

Original Substance moves according to its thoughts; every form and process you see in nature is the visible expression of a thought in Original Substance. As the Formless Stuff thinks of a form, it takes that form; as it thinks of a motion, it makes that motion. That is the way all things were created. We live in a thought world, which is part of a thought universe.

The thought of a moving universe extended throughout Formless Substance, and the Thinking Stuff moving according to that thought, took the form of systems of planets, and maintains that form. Thinking Substance takes the form of its thought, and moves according to the thought. Holding the idea of a circling system of suns and worlds, it takes the form of these bodies, and moves them as it thinks. Thinking the form of a slow-growing oak tree, it moves accordingly, and produces the tree, though centuries may be required to do the work. In creating, the Formless seems to move according to the lines of motion it has established; the thought of an oak tree does not cause the instant formation of a full-grown tree, but it does start in motion the forces which will produce the tree, along established lines of growth.

Every thought of form, held in thinking Substance, causes the creation of the form, but always, or at least generally, along lines of growth and action already established.

The thought of a house of a certain construction, if it were impressed upon Formless Substance, might not cause the instant formation of the house, but it would cause the turning of creative energies already working in trade and commerce into such channels as to result in the speedy building of the house. And if there were no existing channels through which the creative energy could work, then the house would be formed directly from primal substance, without waiting for the slow processes of the organic and inorganic world.

No thought of form can be impressed upon Original Substance without causing the creation of the form.

Man is a thinking center and can originate thought. All the forms that man fashions with his hands must first exist in his thought; he cannot shape a thing until he has thought that thing.

So far man has confined his efforts wholly to the work of his hands; he has applied manual labor to the world of forms, seeking to change or modify those already existing. He has never thought of trying to cause the creation of new forms by impressing his thoughts upon Formless Substance.

When man has a thought-form, he takes material from the forms of nature, and makes an image of the form which is in his mind. He has, so far, made little or no effort to cooperate with Formless Intelligence; to work "with the Father." He has not dreamed that he can "do what he seeth the Father doing." Man reshapes and modifies existing forms by manual labor; he has given no attention to the question whether he may not produce things from Formless Substance by communicating his thoughts to it. We propose to prove that he may do so; to prove that any man or woman may do so, and to show how. As our first step, we must lay down three fundamental propositions.

First, we assert that there is one original formless stuff, or substance, form which all things are made. All the seemingly many elements are but different presentations of one element; all the many forms found in organic and inorganic nature are but different shapes, made from the same stuff. And this stuff is thinking stuff; a thought held in it produces the form of the thought. Thought, in thinking substance, produces shapes. Man is a thinking center, capable of original thought; if man can communicate his thought to original thinking substance, he can cause the creation, or formation, of the thing he thinks about. To summarize this:

There is a thinking stuff from which all things are made, and which, in its original state, permeates, penetrates, and fills the interspaces of the universe.

A thought, in this substance, produces the thing that is imaged by the thought.

Man can form things in his thought and, by impressing his thought upon formless substance, can cause the thing he thinks about to be created.

It may be asked if I can prove these statements; without going into detail, I answer that I can do so, both by logic and experience.

Reasoning back from the phenomena of form and thought, I come to one original thinking substance; reasoning forward from this thinking substance, I come to man's power to cause the formation of the thing he thinks about.

And by experiment, I find the reasoning true; this is my strongest proof.

If one man who reads this book gets rich by doing what it tells him to do, that is evidence in support of my claim; but if every man who does what it tells him to do gets rich, that is positive proof until someone goes through the process and fails. The theory is true until the process fails; this process will not fail, for every man who does exactly what this book tells him to do will get rich.

I have said that men get rich by doing things in a Certain Way, and in order to do so men must become able to think in a certain way.

A man's way of doing things is the direct result of the way he thinks about things.

To do things in a way you want to do them, you will have to acquire the ability to think the way you want to think; this is the first step toward getting rich.

To think what you want to think is to think TRUTH, regardless of appearances.

Every man has the natural and inherent power to think what he wants to think, but it requires far more effort to do so than it does to think the thoughts which are suggested by appearances. To think according to appearances is easy; to think truth regardless of appearances is laborious, and requires the expenditure of more power than any other work man is called upon to perform.

There is no labor from which more people shrink as they do from that of sustained and consecutive thought; it is the hardest work in the world. This is especially true when truth is contrary to appearances. Every appearance in the visible world tends to produce a corresponding form in the mind which observes it, and this can only be prevented by holding the thought of TRUTH.

To look upon the appearance of disease will produce the form of disease in your own mind, and ultimately in your body, unless you hold the thought of the truth, which is that there is no disease; it is only an appearance, and the reality is health.

To look upon the appearance of poverty will produce corresponding forms in your own mind, unless you hold to the truth that there is no poverty; there is only abundance.

To think health when surrounded by the appearances of disease, or to think riches when in the midst of appearances of poverty, requires power; he who acquires this power becomes a MASTER MIND. He can conquer fate; he can have what he wants.

This power can only be acquired by getting hold of the basic fact which is behind all appearances, and that fact is that there is one Thinking Substance, from which and by which all things are made.

Then we must grasp the truth that every thought held in this Substance becomes a form, and that man can so impress his thoughts upon It as to cause them to take form and become visible things.

When we realize this we lose all doubt and fear, for we know that we can create what we want to create; we can get what we want to have, and can become what we want to be. As a first step toward getting rich, you must believe the three fundamental statements given previously in this chapter; in order to emphasize them, I repeat them here:

There is a thinking stuff from which all things are made, and which, in its original state, permeates, penetrates, and fills the interspaces of the universe.

A thought, in this substance, produces the thing that is imaged by the thought.

Man can form things in his thought, and, by impressing his thought upon formless substance, can cause the thing he thinks about to be created.

You must lay aside all other concepts of the universe than this monistic one; you must dwell upon this until it is fixed in your mind and has become your habitual thought. Read these creed statements over and over again; fix every word upon your memory, and meditate upon them until you firmly believe what they say. If a doubt comes to you, cast it aside as a sin. Do not listen to argument against this idea; do not go to churches or lectures where a contrary concept of things is taught or preached. Do not read magazines or books which teach a different idea; if you get mixed up in your faith, all your efforts will be in vain. Do not ask why these things are true, nor speculate as to how they can be true; simply take them on trust. The science of getting rich begins with the absolute acceptance of this faith.

Chapter Four - Taking Action

Understanding Chapter Four

The First Principle in the Science of Getting Rich

1.   Thought is the only power that can produce tangible riches from Formless Substance. How does thought do that? Describe the process in detail?

Everything in the Universe is created by Thought + is a visible expression of a thought created through a known process.

2.   How happy will you be with your life if you continue to impress upon Formless Substance the same thoughts that you are currently impressing upon it? Are you willing to act in a certain way to achieve riches?

I will be much much happier if I can create + achieve so much more of my potential now. I am willing to act in a certain way to achieve it.

3.   What are the three principles about thoughts given in this chapter?

(1) There is a thinking stuff from which all things are made + it permeates, penetrates + fills the interspaces of the Universe.
(2) A thought produces the thing imaged by the thought
(3) I can form things in my thoughts + by putting the thought into the Universe I can create that thing.

Chapter Four Learnings

The most Important principles, concepts and thoughts that I have learned from this Chapter are:

1. _____

_____

_____

_____

2. _____

_____

_____

_____

3. _____

_____

_____

_____

4. _____

_____

_____

_____

5. _____

_____

6. _____

_____

_____

_____

7. _____

_____

_____

_____

8. _____

_____

_____

_____

Chapter Four Learnings

The two most Important principles, concepts and thoughts that I have learned from this Chapter and will use in my life are:

Principle One:

_____

_____

_____

_____

_____

_____

Principle Two:

_____

_____

_____

_____

_____

_____

"Great men and women are who see the spiritual is stronger than any material force; that thoughts rule the world." – Emerson.

"You become what you think about all day long – you cannot think poverty and attain riches,"

Putting the Science of Getting Rich Principles to Work

Recognize: Principle One I recognize in this Chapter is:

_____

_____

_____

_____

_____

Relate: What does this mean to me? What will this principle do for me?

_____

_____

_____

_____

_____

Assimilate: How can I use the principles to achieve my goals/riches?

_____

_____

_____

_____

_____

Apply: How am I going to use it? Action steps. Do It Now!

_____

_____

_____

_____

_____

_____

_____

Putting the Science of Getting Rich Principles to Work

Recognize: Principle Two I recognize in this Chapter is:

_____

_____

_____

_____

_____

_____

Relate: What does this mean to me? What will this principle do for me?

_____

_____

_____

_____

_____

_____

Assimilate: How can I use the principles to achieve my goals/riches?

_____

_____

_____

_____

_____

Apply: How am I going to use it? Action steps. Do It Now!

_____

_____

_____

_____

_____

_____

_____

_____

Internalize The Three Fundamental Statements

Read, write and chant these three fundamental statements over and over again until they are internalized in your consciousness for the next seven days. Meditate upon them until you firmly believe them.

➢ There is a thinking stuff from which all things are made, and which, in its original state, permeates, penetrates, and fills the interspaces of the universe.

➢ A thought in this substance produces the thing that is imagined by the thought.

➢ Man can form things in his thought, and by impressing his thought upon formless substance can cause the thing he think about to be created.

Now, rate your belief in these principles on the scale below.

0   1   2   3   4   5   6   (7)   8   9   10

NO BELIEF   SOME BELIEF   STRONG BELIEF

These are the actions I will take to increase my belief.

I will remind myself of all the many many jobs, things, homes I have created using thought

These are the changes that I will make to my predominate thoughts because of my belief in these three principles.

Don't listen to other's negative thoughts
Stop slagging people off!
Keep positive about my own abilities

What Thoughts Do I Want to Impress Upon Formless Substance?

1. Riches   I have abundance

2. Social   I am well-loved + popular + have high
   integrity. I am talented + trustworthy

3. Family   I am loyal + my family love me +
   are very happy, safe + secure

4. Career   I am a Director of a highly successful
   business

5. Personal development   I am positive and never say
   a bad word about anyone.

6. Spiritual   I have a strong connection to the Divine

7. Relationship - I am a supportive kind loving
   wife. we have a great relationship
   + a wonderful sex-life

8. Travel   I travel all over the world
   having amazing experiences +
   meeting wonderful people +

9. Reputation make a difference. I change
   the world. I am well-known
   globally

10. Talent. I am fantastic at solutions,
    opportunities, communication
    and I excel at everything I do.

As a result of your new learnings list the actions or goals will you are going to accomplish, so that you too can become rich by doing things "in a certain way"

1. DO MY WISH BOOK

2. LISTEN MORE TALK LESS

3. COMMIT TO MY OWN TIME MEDITATING + TALKING TO GOD

4. I WILL PLAN MORE EXPERIENCES

5. I WILL KEEP MY THOUGHTS POSITIVE

6. I WILL HAVE A FRIEND IN GOD.

Chapter Five - Increasing Life

You must get rid of the last vestige of the old idea that there is a Deity whose will it is that you should be poor, or whose purposes may be served by keeping you in poverty.

The Intelligent Substance which is All, and in all, and which lives in All and lives in you, is a consciously Living Substance. Being a consciously living substance, it must have the natural and inherent desire of every living intelligence for increase of life. Every living thing must continually seek for the enlargement of its life, because life, in the mere act of living, must increase itself.

A seed, dropped into the ground, springs into activity, and in the act of living produces a hundred more seeds; life, by living, multiplies itself. It is forever Becoming More; it must do so, if it continues to be at all.

Intelligence is under this same necessity for continuous increase. Every thought we think makes it necessary for us to think another thought; consciousness is continually expanding. Every fact we learn leads us to the learning of another fact; knowledge is continually increasing. Every talent we cultivate brings to the mind the desire to cultivate another talent; we are subject to the urge of life, seeking expression which ever drives us on to know more, to do more, and to be more.

In order to know more, do *more,* and be more we must have *more;* we must have things to use, for we learn, and do, and become, only by using things. We must get rich so that we can live more.

The desire for riches is simply the capacity for larger life seeking fulfillment; every desire is the effort or an unexpressed possibility to come to action. It is power seeking to manifest which causes desire. That which makes you want more money is the same as that which makes the plant grow; it is Life, seeking fuller expression.

The One Living Substance must be subject to this inherent law of all life; it is permeated with the desire to live more; that is why it is under the necessity of creating things.

The One Substance desires to live more in you; hence it wants you to have all the things you can use.

It is the desire of God that you should get rich. He wants you to get rich because he can express himself better through you if you have plenty of things to use in giving him expression. He can live more in you if you have unlimited command of the means of life.

The universe desires you to have everything you want to have.

Nature is friendly to your plans.

Everything is naturally for you.

Make up your mind that this is true.

It is essential, however, that *your purpose should harmonize with the purpose that is in All.*

You must want real life, not merely pleasure or sensual gratification. Life is the performance of function; the individual really lives only when he performs every function, physical, mental and spiritual, of which he is capable, without excess in any.

You do not want to get rich in order to live swinishly, for the gratification of animal desires; that is not life. But the performance of every physical function is a part of life, and no one lives completely who denies the impulses of the body a normal and healthful expression.

You do not want to get rich solely to enjoy mental pleasures, to get knowledge, to gratify ambition, to outshine others, to be famous. ALL these are a legitimate part of life, but the man who lives for the pleasures of the intellect alone will only have a partial life, and he will never be satisfied with his lot.

You do not want to get rich solely for the good of others, to lose yourself for the salvation of mankind, to experience the joys of philanthropy and sacrifice. The joys of the soul are only a part of life, and they are no better or nobler than any other part.

You want to get rich in order that you may eat, drink, and be merry when it is time to do these things; in order that you may surround yourself with beautiful things, see distant lands, feed your mind, and develop your intellect; in order that you may love men and do kind things, and be able to play a good part in helping the world to find truth.

But remember that extreme altruism is no better and no nobler than extreme selfishness; both are mistakes.

Get rid of the idea that God wants you to sacrifice yourself for others, and that you can secure his favor by doing so; God requires nothing of the kind.

What he wants is that you should make the most of yourself, for yourself, and for others; you can help others more by making the most of yourself than in any other way.

You can make the most of yourself only by getting rich; so it is right and praiseworthy that you should give your first and best thought to the work of acquiring wealth.

Remember, however, that the desire of Substance is for all, and its movements must be for more life to all; it cannot be made to work for less life to any, because it is equally in all, seeking riches and life.

Intelligent Substance will make things for you, but it will not take things away from someone else and give them to you.

You must get rid of the thought of competition. You are to create, not to compete for what is created.

You do not have to covet the property of others, or to look at it with wishful eyes; no man has anything of which you cannot have the like, and that without taking what he has away from him.

You are to become a creator, not a competitor; you are going to get what you want, but in such a way that when you get it every other man will have more than he has now.

I am aware that there are men who get a vast amount of money by proceeding in direct opposition to the statements in the paragraph above; let me add a word of explanation here. Men of the plutocratic type who become very rich, do so sometimes purely by their extraordinary ability on the plane of competition; sometimes they unconsciously relate themselves to Substance in its great purposes and movements for the general racial upbuilding through industrial evolution. Rockefeller, Carnegie, Morgan, *et al.,* have been the unconscious agents of the Supreme in the necessary work of systematizing and organizing productive industry; in the end, their work will contribute immensely toward increased life for all. Their day is nearly over; they have organized production, and will soon be succeeded by the agents of the multitude, who will organize the machinery of distribution.

The multi-millionaires are like the monster reptiles of the prehistoric eras; they play a necessary part in the evolutionary process, but the same Power which produced them will dispose of them. And it is well to bear in mind that they have never really been rich; a record of the private lives of most of this class will show that they have really been the most abject and wretched of the poor.

Riches secured on the competitive plane are never satisfactory and permanent; they are yours today and another's tomorrow. Remember, if you are to become rich in a scientific and certain way, you must rise entirely out of the competitive thought. You must never think for a moment that the supply is limited. Just as soon as you begin to think that all the money is being "cornered" and controlled by bankers and others, and that you must exert yourself to get laws passed to stop this process, and so on; in that moment you drop into the competitive mind, and your power to cause creation is gone for the time being; what is worse, you will probably arrest the creative movements you have already instituted.

KNOW that there are countless millions of dollars' worth of gold in the mountains of the earth, not yet brought to light, and know that if there were not, more would be created from Thinking Substance to supply your needs.

KNOW that the money you need will come, even if it is necessary for a thousand men to be led to the discovery of new gold mines tomorrow.

Never look at the visible supply; look always at the limitless riches in Formless Substance, and KNOW that they are coming to you as fast as you can receive and use them. Nobody, by cornering the visible supply, can prevent you from getting what is yours.

So never allow yourself to think for an instant that all the best building *spots* will be taken before you get ready to build your house, unless you hurry. Never worry about the trusts and combines, and get anxious for fear they will soon come to own the whole earth. Never get afraid that you will lose what you want because some other person "beats you to it." That cannot possibly happen; you are not seeking anything that is possessed by anybody else; you are causing what you want to be created from Formless Substance and the supply is without limits. Stick to the formulated statement:

There is a thinking stuff from which all things are made, and which, in its original state, permeates, penetrates, and fills the interspaces of the universe.

A thought, in this substance, produces the thing that is imaged by the thought.

Man can form things in his thought, and, by impressing his thought upon formless substance, can cause the thing he thinks about to be created.

Chapter Five - Taking Action

Understanding Chapter Five

Increasing Life

1.   What does the Intelligent Substance, which is All, and in All, and which lives in All desire for every living intelligence?

To increase life, to multiply, to achieve it's highest potential

2.   Explain what "every desire" is.

Every desire is the effort or unexpressed possibility to come into action.

3.   Does God desire you to get rich? Explain.

Yes. God wants to express himself through me so if I have plenty of things to use it gives him more ways to express himself.

4.   Why are riches secured on the competitive plain never permanent?

Riches created on the competitive plain rely on supply being limited + taking from others.

5.   How do you develop the Creative Mind?

Never think for a moment supply is limited. Know the money you need will come

6.   Explain why there is no scarcity.

There is no scarcity because I am not trying to take from someone that already exists. I am using the Formless substance to create what I want.

"You can be what you want to be;

You can have what you want to have;

You can do what you want to do,

If you want it strong enough,

If you believe it firmly enough

To make it your dominant desire."

Personal intentions carries great power. Intention is what you consciously or unconsciously aim for or establish as a purpose. Your intention, it strong enough, has unbelievable power to create your reality." – George Leonard.

Chapter Five Learnings

The most Important principles, concepts and thoughts that I have learned from this Chapter are:

1. Get rid of all thoughts God wants me to be Poor

2. God wants me to be rich

3. The whole world thrives on growth

4. Desire is unfullfilled potential

5. Being rich is not about competing

6. Being rich is about creating

7. There is no scarcity

8. The Formlen Substance can create more things than I can possibly imagine if I can just think of them it will be so

Chapter Five Learnings

The two most Important principles, concepts and thoughts that I have learned from this Chapter and will use in my life are:

Principle One:

God is abundant + wants me to be rich

Principle Two:

Desire is unfulfilled potential
Balance in all things

"Change your focus, you'll change your future." – Oprah Winfrey.

"Think and Grow Rich" – Napoleon Hill.

"You become your predominate thoughts."

75

Putting the Science of Getting Rich Principles to Work

Recognize: Principle One I recognize in this Chapter is:

God wants me to be rich

Relate: What does this mean to me? What will this principle do for me?

There is nothing stopping me from realizing my highest + fullest potential

Assimilate: How can I use the principles to achieve my goals/riches?

I will think of things I want to achieve
- global status
- fun experiences
- exp fame
- savings

Apply: How am I going to use it? Action steps. Do It Now!

Monthly spending - create a fund for fun, for saving, for paying off mortgage.

Wish Big- all the things I want I know can be mine if I keep focused

Putting the Science of Getting Rich Principles to Work

Recognize: Principle Two I recognize in this Chapter is:

Balance in all things

Relate: What does this mean to me? What will this principle do for me?

I can use money to have fun + never feel guilty because there is more coming.

Assimilate: How can I use the principles to achieve my goals/riches?

I don't have to compare or worry about what other people are doing with their finances or be tight with myself.

Apply: How am I going to use it? Action steps. Do It Now!

I can the key areas to look at:
- generating passive income
- new fun ways to make money
- events, radio, writing books
- More ways to make money from FUN!

My Purpose!

The universe desires you to have everything you want to have.

Nature is friendly to your plans.

Everything is naturally for you.

Make up your mind that this is true.

It is essential that your purpose should harmonize with the purpose that is in ALL

My purpose for getting rich is: to have fun + joy in my life + to spread that joy to others I want to gain + share knowledge & experences meet interesting people + travel the world, throughout my whole life.

My Purpose Harmonizes With The Purpose That Is In All.

My purpose provides increase for myself, physically, mentally, and spiritually in the following ways.

Physically I like to feel strong, happy, active + full of life. Mentally I like to feel I achieve status, name + fame + have a good reputation. I want to be able to provide everything my family needs.

My purpose provides increase for my family in the following ways.

My purpose means I can save for my family buy them the things they want, travel + have fun with them.

78

My purpose provides increase for other loved ones in the following ways.

I can contribute to my friends by giving them time + support + fun + friendship + help them if they need it.

My purpose provides increase for society in the following ways.

I can contribute by more networks, for supporting women, creating more opportunities for Onenen, helping Awaken the whole country + whole word.

Other thoughts about my purpose.

What I Will Do To Make My Life More Complete.

Consider such things such as beauty, travel, feed my mind, love mankind, increasing my mental faculties and doing things you always wanted to do.

Create a Oneness Centre - co-working, project management, digital, creative space for collaborating

Exercise - yoga, massage, swim with dolphins, eat good food.

Travel around in the best most comfortable ways possible + stay in the nicest places.

Have the best quality clothes, house fixtures + fittings.

Have comfy clothes that easily fit me + make me look lovely.

Always look + feel relaxed + calm. Always having the time + resources to do things like give my family first class healthcare.

LOTS OF FUN, NEW, INTERESTING EXPERIENCES - TRAVEL, SING, DANCE ACT, PAINT, RADIO

As a result of your new learnings list the actions or goals will you are going to accomplish, so that you too can become rich by doing things "in a certain way"

1. Then I will open a centre - The Open Heart.

2. I will get a beautiful home with a seaview

3. I will swim with dolphins, surf + scuba dive

4. I will travel the world, singing, dancing, acting + playing

5. I will have a new national radio show, a global TV show, a magazine and write some books.

6. I will always travel in comfort + style + stay in the nicest places.

Chapter Six - How Riches Come To You

When I say that you do not have to drive sharp bargains, I do not mean that you do not have to drive any bargains at all, or that you are above the necessity for having any dealings with your fellow men. I mean that you will not need to deal with them unfairly; you do not have to get something for nothing, *but can give to every man more than you take from him.*

You cannot give every man more in cash market value than you take from him, but you can give him more in use value than the cash value of the thing you take from him. The paper, ink, and other material in this book may not be worth the money you paid for it; but if the ideas suggested by it bring you thousands of dollars, you have not been wronged by those who sold it to you; they have given you a great use value for a small cash value.

Let us suppose that I own a picture by one of the great artists, which, in any civilized community, is worth thousands of dollars. I take it to Baffin Bay, and by "salesmanship" induce an Eskimo to give a bundle of furs worth $500 for it. I have really wronged him, for he has no use for the picture; it has no use value to him; it will not add to his life.

But suppose I give him a gun worth $50 for his furs; then he has made a good bargain. He has use for the gun; it will get him many more furs and much food; it will add to his life in every way; it will make him rich.

When you rise from the competitive to the creative plane, you can scan your business transactions very strictly, and if you are selling any man anything which does not add more to his life than the things he gives you in exchange, you can afford to stop it. You do not have to beat anybody in business. And if you are in a business which does beat people, get out of it at once.

Give every man more in use value than you take from him in cash value; then you are adding to the life of the world by every business transaction.

If you have people working for you, you must take from them more in use value than you pay them in wages; but *you can so organize your business that it will be filled with the principle of advancement,* and so that each employee who wishes to do so may advance a little every day.

You can make your business do for your employees what this book is doing for you. You can so conduct your business that it will be a sort of ladder, by which every employee who will take the trouble may climb to riches by himself, and given the opportunity, if he will not do so it is not your fault.

And finally, because you are to cause the creation of your riches from Formless Substance which permeates all your environment, it does not follow that they are to take shape from the atmosphere and come into being before your eyes.

If you want a sewing machine, for instance, I do not mean to tell you that you are to impress the thought of a sewing machine on Thinking Substance until the machine is formed without hands, in the room where you sit, or elsewhere. But if you want a sewing machine, hold the image of it with positive certainty that it is being made, or is on its way to you. After once forming the thought, have the most absolute and unquestioning faith that the sewing machine is coming; never think of it, or speak of it, in any other way than as being sure to arrive. Claim it as yours.

It will be brought to you by the power of the Supreme Intelligence, acting upon the minds of men. If you live in Maine, it may be that a man will be brought from Texas or Japan to engage in some transaction which will result in your getting what you want.

If so, the whole matter will be as much to that man's advantage as it is to yours.

Do not forget for a moment that the Thinking Substance is through all, in all, communicating with all, and can influence all. The desire of Thinking Substance for fuller life and better living has caused the creation of all the sewing machines already made, and it can cause the creation of millions more, and will, whenever men set it in motion by desire and faith, and by acting in a Certain Way.

You can certainly have a sewing machine in your house; it is just as certain that you can have any other thing or things which you want, and which you will use for the advancement of your own life and the lives of others.

You need not hesitate about asking largely; "It is your Father's good pleasure to give you the kingdom," said Jesus.

Original Substance wants to live all that is possible in you, and wants you to have all that you can or will use for the living of the most abundant life.

If you fix upon your consciousness the fact that the desire you feel for the possession of riches is one with the desire of Omnipotence for more complete expression, your faith becomes invincible.

Once I saw a little boy at a piano, and vainly trying to bring harmony out of the keys; I saw that he was grieved and provoked by his inability to play real music. I asked him the cause of his vexation, and he answered, "I can feel the music in me, but I can't make my hands go right." The music in him was the URGE of Original Substance, containing all the possibilities of all life; all that there is of music was seeking expression through the child.

God, the One Substance, is trying to live and do and enjoy things through humanity. He is saying, "I want hands to build wonderful structures, to play divine harmonies, to paint glorious pictures; I want feet to run my errands, eyes to see my beauties, tongues to tell mighty truths and to sing marvelous songs," and so on.

All that there is of possibility is seeking expression through men. God wants those who can play music to have pianos and every other instrument, and to have the means to cultivate their talents to the fullest extent; He wants those who can appreciate beauty to be able to surround themselves with beautiful things; He wants those who can discern truth to have every opportunity to travel and observe; He wants those who can appreciate dress to be beautifully clothed, and those who can appreciate good food to be luxuriously fed.

He wants all these things because it is Himself that enjoys and appreciates them; it is God who wants to play, and sing, and enjoy beauty, and wear fine clothes, and eat good foods.

"It is God that worketh in you to will and to do," said Paul.

The desire you feel for riches is the Infinite, seeking to express Himself in you as He sought to find expression in the little boy at the piano.

So you need not hesitate to ask largely.

Your part is to focalize and express the desires of God.

This is a difficult point with most people; they retain something of the old idea that poverty and self-sacrifice are pleasing to God. They look upon poverty as a part of the plan, a necessity of nature. They have the idea that God has finished His work, and made all that He can make, and that the majority of men must stay poor because there is not enough to go around. They hold to so much of this erroneous thought that they feel ashamed to ask for wealth; they try not to want more than a very modest competence, just enough to make them fairly comfortable.

I recall now the case of one student who was told that he must get in mind a clear picture of the things he desired, so that the creative thought of them might be impressed on Formless Substance. He was a very poor man, living in a rented house, and having only what he earned from day to day, and he could not grasp the fact that all wealth was his. So, after thinking the matter over, he decided that he might reasonably ask for a new rug for the floor of his best room, and an anthracite coal stove to heat the house during the cold weather. Following the instructions given in this book, he obtained these things in a few months; then it dawned upon him that he had not asked enough. He went through the house in which he lived, and planned all the improvements he would like to make in it; he mentally added a bay window here and a room there, until it was complete in his mind as his ideal home, and then he planned the furnishings.

Holding the whole picture in his mind, he began living in the Certain Way, and moving toward what he wanted; he owns the house now, and is rebuilding it after the form of his mental image. And now, with still larger faith, he is going on to get greater things. It has been unto him according to his faith, and it is so with you and with all of us.

Chapter Six - Taking Action

Understanding Chapter Six

How Riches Come to You

1.   Why must you give every person more in use value than you take from them in cash value?

Because I will add to the world with every transaction - I am not taking away.

2.   How do you create tangible things?

Hold a clear vision
Claim it as mine
Know that it is on the way to me
Never stop ~~thinking of it~~ knowing it will come

3.   Explain why the Universe wants you to have an abundance of all things?

The expression of all the good things in life is God itself experiencing all the fun + joy + lovely things in life.

"We have taken forms and conditions as the starting point of our thought and inferred that they are the cause of our mental states; now we know we have the creative process exactly in reverse and that thoughts and feelings are the causes and forms and conditions are the effects."

Chapter Six Learnings

The most Important principles, concepts and thoughts that I have learned from this Chapter are:

1. Always give in transactions

2. keep a clear vision of material things I want

3. Wish Big

4. Remember God wants us to appreciate the good things in life

5. Remember God wants me to experience the good things in life

6. Remember that the things I want
   are already on the way to me

7. Know that I can always get what
   I really need + want easily

8. Know that I can express myself
   creatively in any way I choose!

Chapter Six Learnings

The two most Important principles, concepts and thoughts that I have learned from this Chapter and will use in my life are:

Principle One:

Keep a clear vision of what you want

Principle Two:

Remember God wants you to express yourself through things

"What you can't see is more powerful than what you can see."

"The Invisible creates the visible."

"Your wealth can only grow to the extent that you can."

Putting the Science of Getting Rich Principles to Work

Recognize: Principle One I recognize in this Chapter is:

keep a Clear vision of what you want

Relate: What does this mean to me? What will this principle do for me?

I need can easily bring the people, resources, time, money, supplies, ideas + things I need at the right time

Assimilate: How can I use the principles to achieve my goals/riches?

I can use a wish book to focus and make my vision clear.
I can talk about what I want + I can write a wish list + put it by my bed.

Apply: How am I going to use it? Action steps. Do It Now!

Make a wish list tonight + put it by my bed.

Putting the Science of Getting Rich Principles to Work

Recognize: Principle Two I recognize in this Chapter is:

Wish big because God wants me to experience life to the max

Relate: What does this mean to me? What will this principle do for me?

Release my limiting beliefs + know I can be a millionaire business person with a good reputation well-loved + happy + stress-free with loyal trustworthy clients, suppliers, partners + staff.

Assimilate: How can I use the principles to achieve my goals/riches?

I can make a clear vision knowing that these things are already coming to me! They are on the way! I'm already a multi-millionaire!

Apply: How am I going to use it? Action steps. Do It Now!

Keep refining + defining + having a clear vision of my goal. Keep making small steps Take every opportunity Every meeting. Keep doing she.says keep loving the whole of Brighton!

My "Ask Largely" List

Wattles says, **"You need not hesitate about asking largely."** Make a list of what you are to "ask largely" for.

I am a multi-millionaire with successful sustainable businesses, an excellent reputation, name + fame, a wonderful space with a seaview + modern funky fixtures. I own property in London, Brighton, SF, Vancouver, India. I travel regularly all over the world. I have a loyal happy + talented team around me. We all love the BRAND - I am the integral part of this BRAND. I am world-famous like Oprah Winfrey or Anita Roddick. I am well-loved + broadcast + create products all over the world. I am a fabulous success!

Make a clear definite picture of what you feel you desire the most from the above list. You may make a Treasure Map of this desire.

My finances are well-managed + I have the best most trustworthy advice. I am part of a fantastic global family. I am the heart of this business. I generate millions for myself + help everyone in the organisation.

Make a Treasure Map of one of your "ask largely" desires.

Well known trusted global brand

Talented Trusted Team

Wonderful high quality Products events speakers courses

Refigure

Well loved + fantastic global + local + national Reputation

Millions of pounds dollars Yen euros are generated for me + others contributing to everyone as a whole

Ethical Sustainable fun happy full of integrity

Sea View

As a result of your new learnings list the actions or goals will you are going to accomplish, so that you too can become rich by doing things "in a certain way"

1.   Make wish lists

2.   Pray to God that I am financially independent

3.   Pray to God that I am a multi-millionaire for the rest of my time on earth.

4.   Pray to God I am financially free!

5.   I can vision my business ideas

6.   I have the best most talented + trustworthy team + nicest clients around me!

Chapter Seven - Gratitude

The illustrations given in the last chapter will have conveyed to the reader the fact that the first step toward getting rich is to convey the idea of your wants to the Formless Substance.

This is true, and you will see that in order to do so it becomes necessary to relate yourself to the Formless Intelligence in a harmonious way.

To secure this harmonious relation is a matter of such primary and vital importance that I shall give some space to its discussion here, and give you instructions which if you will follow them, will be certain to bring you into perfectly unity of mind with God.

The whole process of mental adjustment and atonement can be summed_up in one word, *gratitude*.

First, you believe that there is one Intelligent Substance, from which all things proceed; second, you believe that this Substance gives you everything you desire; and third, you relate yourself to It by a feeling of deep and profound gratitude.

Many people who order their lives rightly in all other ways are kept in poverty by their lack of gratitude. Having received one gift from God, they cut the wires which connect them with Him by failing to make acknowledgment.

It is easy to understand that the nearer we live to the source of wealth, the more wealth we shall receive; and it is easy also to understand that the soul that is always grateful lives in closer touch with God than the one which never looks to Him in thankful acknowledgment.

The more gratefully we fix our minds on the Supreme when good things come to us, the more good things we will receive, and the more rapidly they will come; and the reason simply is that the mental attitude of gratitude draws the mind into closer touch with the source from which the blessings come.

If it is a new thought to you that gratitude brings your whole mind into closer harmony with the creative energies of the universe, consider it well, and you will see that it is true. The good things you already have have come to you along the line of obedience to certain laws. Gratitude will lead your mind out along the ways by which things come; and it will keep you in close harmony with creative thought and prevent you from falling into competitive thought.

Gratitude alone can keep you looking toward the All, and prevent you from falling into the error of thinking of the supply as limited; and to do that would be fatal to your hopes.

There is a Law of Gratitude, and it is absolutely necessary that you should observe the law, if you are to get the results you seek.

The law of gratitude is the natural principle that action and reaction are always equal, and in opposite directions.

The grateful outreaching of your mind in thankful praise to the Supreme *is a liberation or expenditure of force; it cannot fail to reach that to which it is addressed, and the reaction is an instantaneous movement toward you.*

"Draw nigh unto God, and He will draw nigh unto you." That is a statement of psychological truth.

And if your gratitude is strong and constant, the reaction in Formless Substance will be strong and continuous; the movement of the things you want will be always toward you. Notice the grateful attitude that Jesus took; how He always seems to be saying, "I thank Thee, Father, that Thou hearest me." You cannot exercise much power without gratitude; for it is gratitude that keeps you connected with Power.

But the value of gratitude does not consist solely in getting you more blessings in the future. Without gratitude you cannot long keep from dissatisfied thought regarding things as they are.

The moment you permit your mind to dwell with dissatisfaction upon things as they are, you begin to lose ground. You fix attention upon the common, the ordinary, the poor, and the squalid and mean; and your mind takes the form of these things. Then you will transmit these forms or mental images to the Formless, and the common, the poor, the squalid, and mean will come to you.

To permit your mind to dwell upon the inferior is to become inferior and to surround yourself with inferior things.

On the other hand, to fix your attention on the best is to surround yourself with the best, and to become the best.

The Creative Power within us makes us into the image of that to which we give our attention.

We are Thinking Substance, and thinking substance always takes the form of that which of that which it thinks about.

The grateful mind is constantly fixed upon the best; therefore it tends to become the best; it takes the form or character of the best, and will receive the best

Also, faith is born of gratitude. The grateful mind continually expects good things, and expectation becomes faith. The reaction of gratitude upon one's own mind produces faith; and every outgoing wave of grateful thanksgiving increases faith. He who has no feeling of gratitude cannot long retain a living faith; and without a living faith you cannot get rich by the creative method, as we shall see in the following chapters.

It is necessary, then, to cultivate the habit of being grateful for every good thing that comes to you; and to give thanks continuously.

And because all things have contributed to your advancement, you should include all things in your gratitude.

Do not waste time thinking or talking about the shortcomings or wrong actions of plutocrats or trust magnates. Their organization of the world has made your opportunity; all you get really comes to you because of them.

Do not rage against corrupt politicians; if it were not for politicians we should fall into anarchy, and your opportunity would be greatly lessened.

God has worked a long time and very patiently to bring us up to where we are in industry and government, and He is going right on with His work. There is not the least doubt that He will do away with plutocrats, trust magnates, captains of industry, and politicians as soon as they can be spared; but in the meantime, behold they are all very good. Remember that they are all helping to arrange the lines of transmission along which your riches will come to you, and be grateful to them all. This will bring you into harmonious relations with the good in everything, and the good in everything will move toward you.

Chapter Seven - Taking Action
Understanding Chapter Seven
Gratitude

1.   What does Wattles state are the three steps to enter into relationship with the Supreme Power?

① Believe there is one INTELLIGENT SOURCE
② Believe this source gives you EVERYTHING
③ Always give thanks + gratitude
for all the things given to you.

2.   Why is it important to be grateful for all that we receive?

The more grateful we are the
more good things come to us.

3.   How may the Law of Gratitude be stated?

The power of Gratitude is a force that
always reaches the Divine. If your
Gratitude is strong + constant, the gifts
from the Divine will be strong + constant

4.   What happens when you permit your mind to dwell with dissatisfaction upon things as they are?

You will get dragged down to

5.   What is the consequence that "We are Thinking Substance, and thinking substance always takes the form of that which it thinks about?"

If we concentrate on the best, we will
attract the best. And the vice versa
is true.

6.   How is Faith produce?

Faith comes from Gratitude. Being thankful for all we have received + for all that is coming
EXPECT MIRACLES. EXPECT GOOD THINGS

"It is not that you don't have faith – you always have faith.

But what do you have faith in?

The reason you fear poverty is that you have faith that it is possible for you to be poor.

It's time now to develop faith that you can be rich.

"Gratitude must begin with the ONE who created us because we receive the greatest

gift from our Creator – Life." – Don Miguel Ruiz.

Chapter Seven Learnings

The most Important principles, concepts and thoughts that I have learned from this Chapter are:

1. There is one intelligent Source of Creation

2. The Source produces everything

3. Give Thanks + Gratitude always

4. The more grateful we are, the more we get

5. Don't Focus on rubbish, we get dragged down.

6. Faith comes from being Grateful

7. Gratitude must be cultivated + practiced constantly

8. Expect good things to come. Have Faith!

Chapter Seven Learnings

The two most Important principles, concepts and thoughts that I have learned from this Chapter and will use in my life are:

Principle One:

Give Gratitude Always

Principle Two:

Focusing on negative will drag me down.

"When we master gratitude, we can easily receive without feeling guilty because we know by receiving we are giving pleasure to the one who is giving." – Don Miguel Ruiz.

Putting the Science of Getting Rich Principles to Work

Recognize: Principle One I recognize in this Chapter is:

Give Gratitude Always

Relate: What does this mean to me? What will this principle do for me?

Remember everyday, every moment all the fantastic things I have in my life.

Assimilate: How can I use the principles to achieve my goals/riches?

Do not stagnate or get despondent keep planning for the richest the best things to come.

Apply: How am I going to use it? Action steps. Do It Now!

Keep at it with the Wish Book
Express your gratitude every day to the Divine.
Take presents to Sri Bhagavan + Amma
Take presents + cards to all who help me.
Never turn-up empty-handed.

Putting the Science of Getting Rich Principles to Work

Recognize: Principle Two I recognize in this Chapter is:

Do not focus on the negative

Relate: What does this mean to me? What will this principle do for me?

Don't get into a loop being unhappy with my body, clothes, house, sofas street, town.

Assimilate: How can I use the principles to achieve my goals/riches?

Express gratitude for all the wonderful things I have. A strong beautiful youthful body, thankyou for a warm big safe home thankyou for all the wonderful things I have.

Apply: How am I going to use it? Action steps. Do It Now!

Avoid people who moan
Stop moaning
Stop moaning
Stop moaning

The 21 Day Gratitude Process

There are 2 types of gratitude. One is passive. The other one is active or proactive.

Passive Gratitude

We express gratitude in a passive gratitude in a random way. For example we express passive gratitude as a result of seeing, hearing, or reading about some type of tragic event and say something like "Thank God, that that didn't happen to me."

Active Gratitude

We experience active gratitude when we routinely look for people, things, skills, actions, events, and circumstances to be grateful for. For example everyday there are many small things that happen in your life that you can express gratitude for.

Read Chapter Seven once or twice everyday for the entire week until the principles given are assimilated into your being.

"It is necessary then, to cultivate the habit of being grateful for every good thing that comes to you; and to give thanks continuously."

The 21-Day Gratitude Process is designed to make expressing active gratitude a lifetime habit.

The process is simple and effective, it requires only that you sit down once a day, either morning or evening, and with a deep feeling of gratitude you complete the Gratitude Process form for each of the next 21 days.

The 21-Day Gratitude Process consists of completing each these three questions:

1. What are three things that I am grateful that happened today?
2. Why am I grateful for these things?
3. How can I express my gratitude?
4. What is one action that I will take as a result of my gratitude?

Each day complete on of the 21 Day Gratitude Process forms to express your appreciation and gratitude. As the owner of The Science of Getting Rich Action Pack, you may copy. The 21 Day Gratitude Process for you own use.

Here is a list of a few ideas for expressing gratitude.

1. Small things that have made a difference to your life today.
2. Something that you appreciate about the money you spend or received today.
3. People, teachers, mentors that you appreciate for helping you develop mentally, physically and spiritually.
4. Appreciating your life and what it means to be alive.
5. Things in the world that express – love, truth, beauty, or perfection.

The 21-Day Gratitude Process

Day: 1		Date: 22 OCT 2013	
I'm Grateful For:	Why am I Grateful?	How Can I Express This Gratitude?	One Action I Can Take as a Result.
~~Free Acupuncture~~			
Free Acupuncture	love + care from Helen	give a plant	gave the plant
The Meeting	happy for Luis's skills	hanging out	say thankyou - find him work
My husband	he loves me	Say thankyou	Phone him later
My mum	she loves me	buy her IPAD mini	call her now
My sister	she loves me	text her more	text her now

Day: 2		Date: 23 OCT 2013	
I'm Grateful For:	Why am I Grateful?	How Can I Express This Gratitude?	One Action I Can Take as a Result.
Luis selling me	I am give to my mum	Pay him on time	Say Thankyou
Friends like Maddy	for thinking highly of my work	Sending a Xmas card	Meet her later.
Gina for helping me	Getting a discount	Pran an to the lab	Be grateful of apple purchasing
Charlie	Being kind	Being nice + patient	waiting no charging
Natalee	for being my friend	Be nice at Teox	Be kind to her parents

Day: 3		Date: 24 OCT 2013	
I'm Grateful For:	Why am I Grateful?	How Can I Express This Gratitude?	One Action I Can Take as a Result.
~~Charlie~~	for negoti		
Charlie	for negotiating	Saying thankyou	Do the job effectively
Chris	for loving me	saying I love you	Being kind
Natalie	for tweeting	Supporting Teox	Being nice
Caila	for being generous	Texting her	Buying her presents
Samantha	for being a friend	being kind	feeling her tomorrow

109

The 21-Day Gratitude Process

Day: 4		Date: 25 OCt 2013	
I'm Grateful For:	Why am I Grateful?	How Can I Express This Gratitude?	One Action I Can Take as a Result.
Samantha	her friendship	Send her a card	Write Text her
All my friends	& I feel valued	Send cards	& Tweet!
My husband	Caring home	Be nice	Say Do sex!
My new friend	giving advice	Text him	Say thankyou
To God	For loving me	Pranam	Do it now!

Day: 5		Date: 26 Oct 2013	
I'm Grateful For:	Why am I Grateful?	How Can I Express This Gratitude?	One Action I Can Take as a Result.
Nat + Fit	Asking me to be proper person	Dinner	Do the maths
Chris	Being patient	letting him sleep	Les Nagging
Joanna	For cleaning	Say thankyou	Stop charging she
Woman @ BT	Giving Mum discount	Did Say thanks	Do the survey
Paperchase person	Giving me stickers	say thankyou	Be grateful.

Day: 6		Date: 27 Oct 2013	
I'm Grateful For:	Why am I Grateful?	How Can I Express This Gratitude?	One Action I Can Take as a Result.
My Reiki students	for trusting me	Saying thankyou	emailing thanks
Lorna	for listening	saying thankyou	Texting her
Spice rutiment	for the lovely food	ordering again	say thankyou
God, Angels	for helping me	Thankyou	Using the
Sri Amma Bhagavan	do the workshop	Thankyou	Money for India.

The 21-Day Gratitude Process

Day: ⑦		Date: 28 OCt 2013	
I'm Grateful For:	Why am I Grateful?	How Can I Express This Gratitude?	One Action I Can Take as a Result.
Rhona	helping me /advice	Say thank you	Do my homework
Charlie	for agreeing costs	do a good job	answer him today
Chris	cuddles + food	say thank you	make him tea
Luis	for considering work	Pay him bonus	give him questions + the stuff
Amma Bhagavan	for bringing me people	say thank you	take notebooks.

Day: ⑧		Date: 29 Oct 2013	
I'm Grateful For:	Why am I Grateful?	How Can I Express This Gratitude?	One Action I Can Take as a Result.
Estate agents	asking me to view	Say thank you	turn up on time
Chris	getting me tix	Say thank you	Be nice
Rachael	for giving me tix	Say thank you	send link.
Rhona	for helping me focus	say thank you	listen + do
Amma Bhagavan	for giving healing	helping me	Say thank you

Day: ⑨		Date: 30 OCt 2013	
I'm Grateful For:	Why am I Grateful?	How Can I Express This Gratitude?	One Action I Can Take as a Result.
Amma Bhagavan	All the gifts	Pranam	Say thank you
The Yuiters	for the coming	Say thank you	Go again in Jan
Sue Cross	for the support	Say thank you	offer petrol money
Chris	for the fun	Say thank you	Give more
Estate agents	Showing me	Say thank you	Say No thanks
Natalie	for the friendship	Give her £980	Just do it

The 21-Day Gratitude Process

Day: ⑩		Date: 31 OCt 2013	
I'm Grateful For:	Why am I Grateful?	How Can I Express This Gratitude?	One Action I Can Take as a Result.
Ben	For friendship	Say thanks	Be nice.
Estate agents	showing me around	Say thankyou	Be nice to them
Charlie	for being nice	Do a good job	finish nicely
Natalie	for fun + friendship	Be nice	Say thankyou
Chris	for cooking	Say thankyou	Be nice
Amma Bhagavan	for helping me do a OM	Say thankyou	Meditate

Day: ⑪		Date: 1 NOV 2013	
I'm Grateful For:	Why am I Grateful?	How Can I Express This Gratitude?	One Action I Can Take as a Result.
Isha	The Online OM	Say thankyou	Straight away
Chris	Cooking meals	Say thankyou	Make cups of tea
Amma Bhagavan	Guiding me today	Pranam	Relax + let go
Tejasa	For helping me	Giving her pads	Be the best kamba
Lorna	for the bears	Say thankyer	Be a good friend
Charlie	for paying me on time	Say thankyou	Do a good job.

Day: ⑫		Date: 2 NOV 2013	
I'm Grateful For:	Why am I Grateful?	How Can I Express This Gratitude?	One Action I Can Take as a Result.
Lorna	Coming to Salisbury	Say thankyou	Be her friend
Mark	organising	Email him	Say thanks for call
Julie	Coming to OM	Say thankyou	Send her CD
Chris	being here	comfort	Be nice
Lewis	for doing the work making (you	Be kind.

The 21-Day Gratitude Process

Day: (13)		Date: 3 Nov 2013	
I'm Grateful For:	Why am I Grateful?	How Can I Express This Gratitude?	One Action I Can Take as a Result.
Nat + Ant	Good friendship	Buy a present	See them more
Chris	loving me	Be nice	Buy him dinner
Sri AnnaBhagavan	All the gifts	Pranam	Remember them
Rhona	Help with finances	Say thankyou	do the homework
Mum	loving me	Give her iPad	Ring her more.

Day: (14)		Date: 4 Nov 2013	
I'm Grateful For:	Why am I Grateful?	How Can I Express This Gratitude?	One Action I Can Take as a Result.
Chris	doing the work	hanging out	Pay him on time
Milany	paying my travel	Say thanks	Reply promptly
Chris	cooking dinne	Loving him	Being nice
Deksha givers	for coming	say thankyou	Be nice
Maddy	meeting up	Say thankyou	email her

Day: (15)		Date: 5 Nov 2013	
I'm Grateful For:	Why am I Grateful?	How Can I Express This Gratitude?	One Action I Can Take as a Result.
Lorna	Coming to london	Say thankyou	Email her
Indian Restaurant	food was fab	Go again	Add comment for 4square
Rachel Blackman	Brilliant play	Tell people	Recommend it
Sri AnnaBhagavan	working through me	Pranam	Take them honey
Helen	offer friendship	Offer to help	send a card.
Matthew	fixing my back	Say thanks	Tweet.

113

The 21-Day Gratitude Process

Day: 16		Date: 6 NOV 2013	
I'm Grateful For:	Why am I Grateful?	How Can I Express This Gratitude?	One Action I Can Take as a Result.
Sri Amma Bhagavan	Guiding me	Pranam	Loving them
Helen	Acupuncture	Paying her	Thanking her
My Body	for carrying me	Resting	Protect it
Luis	for being a friend	Buy him lunch	meet him on time
Chris	Coming home	Buy him shoes	Be nice.

Day: 17		Date: 7 NOV 2013	
I'm Grateful For:	Why am I Grateful?	How Can I Express This Gratitude?	One Action I Can Take as a Result.
Luis	Doing the work	Pay him	hang out
Chris	for my bath presents	ring him	listen to him
My body	for being strong	rest	nurture it
Sri Amma Bhagavan	Guiding me	meditate	thank them
Rhona	last minute coaching	Be kind	Be nice.

Day: 18		Date: 8 NOV 2013	
I'm Grateful For:	Why am I Grateful?	How Can I Express This Gratitude?	One Action I Can Take as a Result.
My new bra	It looks great	Buying it	looking after it
Amma Bhagavan	for guiding me	Pranam	meditate
Hot yoga	for providing	Say thank you	Go on Sunday
My body	Being strong + healthy	feed it	Rest/hot bath
All my stuff	For Being here for me to use	Fix it	Look after it

The 21-Day Gratitude Process

Day: 19		Date: 9 NOV 2013	
I'm Grateful For:	Why am I Grateful?	How Can I Express This Gratitude?	One Action I Can Take as a Result.

Day: 20		Date: 10 NOV 2013	
I'm Grateful For:	Why am I Grateful?	How Can I Express This Gratitude?	One Action I Can Take as a Result.

Day: 21		Date: 11 NOV 2013	
I'm Grateful For:	Why am I Grateful?	How Can I Express This Gratitude?	One Action I Can Take as a Result.

As a result of your new learnings list the actions or goals will you are going to accomplish, so that you too can become rich by doing things "in a certain way"

1. _____

    _____

    _____

    _____

2. _____

    _____

    _____

    _____

3. _____

    _____

    _____

    _____

4. _____

    _____

    _____

    _____

5. _____

    _____

    _____

    _____

6. _____

    _____

    _____

Chapter Eight - Thinking In The Certain Way

Turn back to Chapter Six and read again the story of the man who formed a mental image of his house, and you will get a fair idea of the initial step toward getting rich. You must form a clear and definite mental picture of what you want; you cannot transmit an idea unless you have it yourself.

You must have it before you can give it; and many people fail to impress Thinking Substance because they have themselves only a vague and misty concept of the things they want to do, to have, or to become.

It is not enough that you should have a general desire for wealth "to do good with"; everybody has that desire.

It is not enough that you should have a wish to travel, see things, live more, etc. Everybody has those desires also. If you were going to send a telegram message to a friend, you would not send the letters of the alphabet in their order, and let him construct the message for himself; nor would you take words at random from the dictionary. You would send a coherent sentence; one which meant something. When you try to impress your wants upon Substance, remember that it must be done by a coherent statement; you must know what you want, and be definite.

You can never get rich, or start the creative power into action, by sending out unformed longings and vague desires.

Go over your desires just as the man I have described went over his house; see just what you want, and get a clear mental picture of it as you wish it to look when you get it.

That clear mental picture you must have continually in mind, as the sailor has in mind the port toward which he is sailing the ship; you must keep your face toward it all the time. You must no more lose sight of it than the navigator loses sight of the compass.

It is not necessary to take exercises in concentration, nor to set apart special times for prayer and affirmation, nor to "go into the silence," nor to do occult stunts of any kind. These things are well enough, but all you need is to know what you want, and to want it badly enough so that it will stay in your thoughts.

Spend as much of your leisure time as you can in contemplating your picture, but no one needs to take exercises to concentrate his mind on a thing which he really wants; it is the things you do not really care about which require effort to fix your attention upon them.

And unless you really want to get rich, so that the desire is strong enough to hold your thoughts directed to the purpose as the magnetic pole holds the needle of the compass, it will hardly be worth while for you to try to carry out the instructions given in this book.

The methods herein set forth are for people whose desire for riches is strong enough to overcome mental laziness and the love of ease, and make them work.

The more clear and definite you make your picture, then, and the more you dwell upon it, bringing out all its delightful details, the stronger your desire will be; and the stronger your desire, the easier it will be to hold your mind fixed upon the picture of what you want.

Something more is necessary, however, than merely to see the picture clearly. If that is all you do, you are only a dreamer, and will have little or no power for accomplishment.

Behind your clear vision must be the purpose to realize it; to bring it out in tangible expression.

And, behind this purpose must be an invincible and unwavering FAITH that the thing is already yours; that it is "at hand" and you have only to take possession of it.

Live in the new house, mentally, until it takes form around you physically. In the mental realm, enter at once into full enjoyment of the things you want.

"Whatsoever things, ye ask for when ye pray, believe that ye receive them, and ye shall have them," said Jesus.

See the things you want as if they were actually around you all the time; see yourself as owning and using them. Make use of them in imagination just as you will use them when they are your tangible possessions. Dwell upon your mental, picture until it is clear and distinct, and then take the Mental Attitude of Ownership toward everything in that picture. Take possession of it, in mind, in the full faith that it is actually yours. Hold to this mental ownership; do not waver for an instant in the faith that it is real. And remember what was said in a preceding chapter about gratitude; be as thankful for it all the time as you expect to be when it has taken form. The man who can sincerely thank God for the things which as yet he owns only in imagination, has real faith. He will get rich; he will cause the creation of whatsoever he wants.

You do not need to pray repeatedly for the things you want; it is not necessary to tell God about it every day.

"Use not vain repetitions as the heathen do," said Jesus to His pupils, "for your Father knoweth that ye have need of these things before ye ask Him."

Your part is to intelligently formulate your desire for the things which make for a larger life, and to get these desires arranged into a coherent whole; and then to impress this Whole Desire upon the Formless Substance, which has the power and the will to bring you what you want.

You do not make this impression by repeating strings of words; you make it by holding the vision with unshakable PURPOSE to attain it, and with steadfast FAITH that you do attain it.

The answer to prayer is not according to your faith while you are talking but according to your faith while you are working.

You cannot impress the mind of God by having a special Sabbath day set apart to tell Him what you want, and then forgetting Him during the rest of the week. You cannot impress Him by having special hours to go into your closet and pray, if you then dismiss the matter from your mind until the hour of prayer comes again.

Oral prayer is well enough, and has its effect, especially upon yourself, in clarifying your vision and strengthening your faith; but it is not your oral petitions which get you what you want. In order to get rich you do not need a "sweet hour of prayer"; you need to "pray without ceasing." And by prayer I mean holding steadily to your vision, with the purpose to cause its creation into solid form, and the faith that you are doing so.

"Believe that ye *receive* them."

The whole matter turns on receiving, once you have clearly formed your vision. When you have formed it, it is well to make an oral statement, addressing the Supreme in reverent prayer; and from that moment you must, in mind, receive what you ask for. Live in the new house; wear the fine clothes; ride in the automobile; go on the journey, and confidently plan for greater journeys. Think and speak of all the things you have asked for in terms of actual present ownership. Imagine an environment, and a financial condition exactly as you want them, and live all the time in that imaginary environment and financial condition. Mind, however, that you do not do this as a mere dreamer and castle builder; hold to the FAITH that the imaginary is being realized, and to the PURPOSE to realize it. Remember that it is faith and purpose in the use of the imagination which make the difference between the scientist and the dreamer. And having learned this fact, it is here that you must learn the proper use of the Will.

Chapter Eight - Taking Action
Understanding Chapter Eight
Thinking in a Certain Way

1.   What is the first step in making an impression on the Thinking Substance?

Get a clear vision of what I want

2.   What does Wattles suggest that we do with our leisure time? Why is this important?

Keep thinking about the vision of what I want, with passion + clear intent.

3.   How do you internalize the thing that you want?

Use my imagination to clearly picture myself using + doing the things I want.

"All disappointments and failures are a result of endeavouring to think one thing and produce another,"

"You have absolute control over but one ting, and that is your thoughts. This is the most significant and inspiring of all the facts known to mankind." – T. Troward.

Chapter Eight Learnings

The most Important principles, concepts and thoughts that I have learned from this Chapter are:

1. Have a Clear Vision of what I want

2. Keep thinking about my vision as if I already have it

3. Use my imagination to keep making my vision even more real

4. Do not waver in my faith it is coming. It exists now!

5. No need to keep asking God

_____

_____

6. _____

_____

_____

_____

7. _____

_____

_____

_____

8. _____

_____

_____

_____

Chapter Eight Learnings

The two most Important principles, concepts and thoughts that I have learned from this Chapter and will use in my life are:

Principle One:

_____

_____

_____

_____

_____

_____

_____

Principle Two:

_____Make a clear vision_____

_____

_____

_____

_____

_____

"Wealth is a product of an individuals capacity to think." – Ayn Rand.

"All that a man calls his world, is but a picture of his thoughts." – E. Cutis Hopkins.

"Thoughts are things." – Prentice Mulford.

Putting the Science of Getting Rich Principles to Work

Recognize: Principle One I recognize in this Chapter is:

_____

_____

_____

_____

_____

_____

Relate: What does this mean to me? What will this principle do for me?

_____

_____

_____

_____

_____

_____

Assimilate: How can I use the principles to achieve my goals/riches?

_____

_____

_____

_____

_____

Apply: How am I going to use it? Action steps. Do It Now!

_____

_____

_____

_____

_____

_____

_____

_____

Putting the Science of Getting Rich Principles to Work

Recognize: Principle Two I recognize in this Chapter is:

_____

_____

_____

_____

_____

Relate: What does this mean to me? What will this principle do for me?

_____

_____

_____

_____

_____

_____

Assimilate: How can I use the principles to achieve my goals/riches?

_____

_____

_____

_____

Apply: How am I going to use it? Action steps. Do It Now!

_____

_____

_____

_____

_____

_____

The Science of Getting Rich

Steps to Riches

Use These Steps For Getting Rich

1.   To do things in a way that you want to do them; you will have to acquire the ability to think the way that you want to think – Regardless of Appearances.

2.   You must believe these three presuppositions:

   a) There is a thinking stuff from which all things are made, and which, in its original state, permeates, penetrates, and fills the interspaces of the universe.

   b) A thought, in this substance, produces the thing that is imaged by the thought.

   c) Man can form things in his thought, and, by impressing his thought upon formless substance, can cause the thing he thinks about to be created.

   Repeat these statements with emotion until you have FAITH in their reality.

3.   Convey the idea of what you want to the Formless Substance. Your purpose must harmonize with the purpose which is in All in All.

4.   Hold a clear and definite image of your desire with the most positive certainty that it is on its way to you.

   a) Have absolute unquestioning FAITH. Never speak of it in any way other than it is sure to arrive. Claim it as already yours.

   b) You must know your desire will come for Original Substance and will not be taken away from any one else. There is to be no competition. What you want will come from the invisible Formless Substance.

   c) The creative power within you makes you into the image of that which you give your attention. You are thinking substance and thinking substance always takes the form of that which it thinks.

   d) Spend as much of your leisure time contemplating a detailed representation of your desire. Do this with an immense desire. Be emotional. The more clear and definite you make your picture, then, and the more you dwell upon it, bringing out all its delightful details, the stronger will be your desire. And the easier it will be to hold your attention on it.

   e) Fix in your consciousness the fact that the desire you feel for the procession of riches is one with the desire of Original Substance (which is Omnipotence, Omniscient and Omnipresent) for more complete expression and your FAITH will be invincible.

f) Behind your clear vision must be the purpose to realize it; to bring it out in tangible expression.

g) And, behind this purpose must be an invincible and unwavering FAITH that the thing is already yours; that it is "at hand" and, you, have only to take possession of it.

h) See the things you want as if they were actually around you all the time; see yourself as owning and using them. Make use of them in imagination just as you will use them when they are your tangible possessions. Dwell upon your mental, picture until it is clear and distinct, and then take the Mental Attitude of Ownership toward everything in that picture. Take possession of it, in mind, in the full faith that it is actually yours. Hold to this mental ownership; do not waver for an instant in the faith that it is real.

i) Believe that there is One Intelligence Substance and that this Substance gives you everything you desire.

j) Relate yourself to the One Intelligence Substance with a deep feeling of Gratitude. Give thanks continually for every good that comes to you. Cultivate the habit Gratitude. The person who can sincerely thank God for the things that as yet they owns only in imagination, has real faith. They will get rich; they will cause the creation of whatsoever they want.

5)	Make a passionate oral statement of what you want; ending with a statement of gratitude.

6)	Use your will.

a) You do not have to apply will power to anything or anybody outside of yourself. Use your will to compel yourself to think the right things. Things are not brought into being by thinking about their opposite. Use your will to keep your mind fixed with FAITH and PURPOSE on the vision of what you want.

b) Fix your attention upon your mental picture of riches to the exclusion of all that may tend to dim or obscure the vision.

7)	Connect thought with personal action. To receive what you want when it comes you must ACT NOW upon the people and things in your present environment. Do everyday all that can be done that day and do it in an efficient manner. Every act can be made strong and efficient by holding your vision in mind while you are doing it and putting the whole process of your FAITH and Purpose into it.

a) It should be the work of your leisure hours to use your imagination on the details of your vision, and to contemplate them until they are firmly fixed upon your memory

b) If you wish speedy results, spend practically all your spare time in this practice. By continuous contemplation you will get the picture of what you want, even to the smallest details, so firmly fixed upon your mind, and so completely transferred to the mind of Formless Substance, that in your working hours you need only to mentally refer to the picture to stimulate your faith and purpose, and cause your best effort to be put forth. Contemplate your picture in your leisure hours until your consciousness is so full of it that you can grasp it instantly. You will become so enthused with its bright promises that the mere thought of it will call forth the strongest energies of your whole being.

8) Convey the impression of advancement with everything you do.

a) You are a creative center, from which increase is given off to all. Be sure of this, and convey assurance of the fact to every man, woman, and child with whom you come in contact. No matter how small the transaction, even if it be only the selling of a stick of candy to a little child, put into it the thought of increase, and make sure that the customer is impressed with the thought.

b) You can convey this impression by holding the unshakable faith that you, yourself, are in the Way of Increase; and by letting this faith inspire, fill, and permeate every action.

9) Be more than your current place. The person who is certain to advance is the one who is too big for their place, and who has a clear concept of what they want to be; who know that they can become what they want to be, and who is determined to BE what they want to be.

a) Do not wait for an opportunity to be all that you want to be; when an opportunity, to be more than you are now is presented and you feel impelled toward it, take it. It will be the first step toward a greater opportunity

b) There is no such thing possible in this universe as a lack of opportunities for the man who is living the advancing life.

The combined mental and personal action above is infallible; it cannot fail. Every man or women, who follow these instructions steadily, perseveringly and to the letter, will get rich. The Law of Increase of Life is as mathematically certain in its operation as the law of gravitation. Getting rich is an exact science.

Study and internalize these steps to riches.

As a result of your new learnings list the actions or goals will you are going to accomplish, so that you too can become rich by doing things "in a certain way"

1. Create a clear list of what I want

2. Make the wish book

3. Create statements, wishes + prayers for God – ending with Thankyou!

4. Every day be Grateful instead of moaning

5. Know that the riches, experiences, resources, time, people + everything I want + need to be successful + rich is already THERE.

6. Grab opportunities that make my heart sing!

Chapter Nine - How To Use The Will

To set about getting rich in a scientific way, you do not try to apply your will power to anything outside of yourself.

You have no right to do so, anyway.

It is wrong to apply your will to other men and women, in order to get them to do what you wish done.

It is as flagrantly wrong to coerce people by mental power as it is to coerce them by physical power. If compelling people by physical force to do things for you reduces them to slavery, compelling them by mental means accomplishes exactly the same thing; the only difference is in methods.

If taking things from people by physical force is robbery, then taking things by mental force is robbery also; there is no difference in principle.

You have no right to use your will power upon another person, even "for his own good"; for you do not know what is for his good.

The science of getting rich does not require you to apply power or force to any other person, in any way whatsoever. There is not the slightest necessity for doing so; indeed, any attempt to use your will upon others will only tend to defeat your purpose.

You do not need to apply your will to things, in order to compel them to come to you.

That would simply be trying to coerce God, and would be foolish and useless, as well as irreverent.

You do not have to compel God to give you good things, any more than you have to use your will power to make the sun rise.

You do not have to use your will power to conquer an unfriendly deity, or to make stubborn and rebellious forces do your bidding.

Substance is friendly to you, and is more anxious to give you what you want than you are to get it.

To get rich, you need only to use your will power upon yourself.

When you know what to think and do, then you must use your will to compel yourself to think and do the right things. That is the legitimate use of the will in getting what you want—to use it in holding yourself to the right course. Use you will to keep yourself thinking and acting in the Certain Way.

Do not try to project your will, or your thoughts, or your mind out into space, to "act" on things or people.

Keep your mind at home; it can accomplish more there than elsewhere.

Use your mind to form a mental image of what you want, and to hold that vision with faith and purpose; and use your will to keep your mind working the Right Way.

The more steady and continuous your faith and purpose, the more rapidly you will get rich, because you will make only POSITIVE impressions upon Substance, and you will not neutralize or offset them by negative impressions.

The picture of your desires, held with faith and purpose, is taken up by the Formless, and permeates it to great distances,—throughout the universe, for all I know.

As this impression spreads, all things are set moving toward its realization; every living thing, every inanimate thing, and the things yet uncreated, are stirred toward bringing into being that which you want. All forces begins to be exerted in that direction; all things begin to move toward you. The minds of people, everywhere, are influenced toward doing the things necessary to the fulfilling of your desires, and they work for you, unconsciously.

But you can check all this by starting a negative impression in the Formless Substance. Doubt or unbelief is as certain to start a movement away from you as faith and purpose are to start one toward you. It is by not understanding this that most people who try to make use of "mental science" in getting rich make their failure. Every hour and moment you spend in giving heed to doubts and fears, every hour you spend in worry, every hour in which your soul is possessed by unbelief, sets a current away from you in the whole domain of intelligent Substance. All the promises are unto them that believe, and unto them only. Notice how insistent Jesus was upon this point of belief; and now you know the reason why.

Since belief is all important, it behooves you to guard your thoughts; as your beliefs will be shaped to a very great extent by the things you observe and think about, it is important that you should command your attention.

And here the will comes into use; for it is by your will that you determine upon what things your attention shall be fixed.

If you want to become rich, you must not make a study of poverty.

Things are not brought into being by thinking about their opposites. Health is never to be attained by studying disease and thinking about disease; righteousness is not to be promoted by studying sin and thinking about sin; and no one ever got rich by studying poverty and thinking about poverty.

Medicine as a science of disease has increased disease; religion as a science of sin has promoted sin, and economics as a study of poverty will fill the world with wretchedness and want.

Do not talk about poverty; do not investigate it, or concern yourself with it. Never mind what its causes are; you have nothing to do with them.

What concerns you is the cure.

Do not spend your time in charitable work, or charity movements; all charity only tends to perpetuate the wretchedness it aims to eradicate.

I do not say that you should be hard-hearted or unkind, and refuse to hear the cry of need; but you must not try to eradicate poverty in any of the conventional ways. Put poverty behind you, and put all that pertains to it behind you, and "make good."

Get rich; that is the best way you can help the poor.

And you cannot hold the mental image which is to make you rich if you fill your mind with pictures of poverty. Do not read books or papers which give circumstantial accounts of the wretchedness of the tenement dwellers, of the horrors of child labor, and so on. Do not read anything which fills your mind with gloomy images of want and suffering.

You cannot help the poor in the least by knowing about these things; and the wide-spread knowledge of them does not tend at all to do, away with poverty.

What tends to do away with poverty is not the getting of pictures of poverty into your mind, but getting pictures of wealth into the minds of the poor.

You are not deserting the poor in their misery when you refuse to allow your mind to be filled with pictures of that misery.

Poverty can be done away with, not by increasing the number of well-to-do people who think about poverty, but by increasing the number of poor people who purpose with faith to get rich.

The poor do not need charity; they need inspiration. Charity only sends them a loaf of bread to keep them alive in their wretchedness, or gives them an entertainment to make them forget for an hour or two, but inspiration will cause them to rise out of their misery. If you want to help the poor, demonstrate to them that they can become rich; prove it by getting rich yourself.

The only way in which poverty will ever be banished from this world is by getting a large and constantly increasing number of people to practice the teachings of this book.

People must be taught to become rich by creation, not by competition.

Every man who becomes rich by competition throws down behind him the ladder by which he rises, and keeps others down, but every man who gets rich by creation opens a way for thousands to follow him, and inspires them to do so.

You are not showing hardness of heart or an unfeeling disposition when you refuse to pity poverty, or think or talk about it, or to listen to those who do talk about it. Use your will power to keep your mind OFF the subject of poverty, and to keep it fixed with faith and purpose ON the vision of what you want.

Chapter Nine - Taking Action
Understanding Chapter Nine
How to Use the Will

1. Why do you have no right to apply your will upon others?

    For I do not know what is best for them

2. How is the correct way to apply your will?

    I only need to use my willpower on myself

3. Why must you guard your thoughts?

    Doubt will create failure

4. How does the science of getting rich say we should get rid of poverty?

    No-one ever got rich by studying poverty to get rich honest is the best way to help the poor.

"It should never be your endeavour to take possession of the mind of another – use your will only on yourself."

Chapter Nine Learnings

The most Important principles, concepts and thoughts that I have learned from this Chapter are:

1. Keep your mind off poverty

2. Poverty can only be eradicated by inspiring people to be rich

3. Creation can only create wealth not competition

4. By becoming rich I can help others be rich

5. By keeping a clear vision I help the whole of humanity

6. Do not impose your will on others

7. Do not apply force on others

8. Do not try to coerce God – !

Chapter Nine Learnings

The two most Important principles, concepts and thoughts that I have learned from this Chapter and will use in my life are:

Principle One:

Do not try to impose your will on another.

Principle Two:

Keep your mind off poverty

"The real secret of power is our consciousness of power, because whatever we consciously use our will to hold in our mind is invariably manifest in the objective world."

Putting the Science of Getting Rich Principles to Work

Recognize: Principle One I recognize in this Chapter is:

Do not impose your will on another.

Relate: What does this mean to me? What will this principle do for me?

I can not + should not nag my husband into losing weight, even if I think it is for his "own good". I must not critisize his lack of funds or ways of making money.

Assimilate: How can I use the principles to achieve my goals/riches?

I can concentrate on my own fitness + my own education about making money. We can both plan how we will spend our riches, + how riches will generate more riches for our future happiness

Apply: How am I going to use it? Action steps. Do It Now!

I will stop judging my husband's eating habits + make sure he also benefits from my "good way with money". I will generate so many income streams, well-managed - that we can both enjoy the work we do without worrying about money.

Putting the Science of Getting Rich Principles to Work

Recognize: Principle Two I recognize in this Chapter is:

Keep your mind off Poverty

Relate: What does this mean to me? What will this principle do for me?

Stop thinking there is lack.
Be generous
Remember there are many ways
to be wealthy I do not need to
take from others or be in competition

Assimilate: How can I use the principles to achieve my goals/riches?

I can now stop trying to take from
others such as charging too much
or asking for too big a salary.
I can generate more passive income
streams + get save for my future.

Apply: How am I going to use it? Action steps. Do It Now!

I am ready to be rich. I will know I
am rich when I am earning at least
£100,000 a year + my outgoings
are still only $ only a quarter of
that. I am making 100% of
what I earn spend. Avoid people who
are trapped in POVERTY - THINKING
Hang around wealthy people to
be RICH! I am 140 always debt free.

The Seven Day Mental Diet for Right Use of Will

One of the most important things in your life is the "Mental Diet" that you habitually live. The "food" which you provide to your mind determines the whole character of your life.

The thoughts that you think, the subjects that you put your attention on determine what you will be, do and have as well as what your surroundings will be.

Look at these areas of your life, your finances, your health, your relationships, your spiritual life and your social life – the results that you are getting in each of these domains is a direct result of what you have thought in the past.

In other words, your financial success is entirely a result of the thoughts and feelings which you have accepted in the past by the habitual tone of your past thinking.

Your financial future today, tomorrow, next week, next year and the rest of your life will be entirely conditioned by the thoughts and feelings which you CHOOSE to entertain from now forwards.

You cannot think lack and experience abundance. To change any of these areas of your life you must change your habitual thoughts in that area.

This course deals specifically with your financial life. The way to make a change to your current financial experience is to change your thoughts as given in this course.

Using The Seven Day Mental Diet to the Right Use of the Will is critical to your future. In fact your Mental Diet is one of the most important aspects in your life.

The Seven Day Mental Diet to the Right Use of the Will will begin to train you in the habit of thought selection and thought control. Continued use of the "diet" will form a new habit of thought control both consciously and unconsciously.

Make up your mind to follow through with this mental process. Spend one week totally concentrating on building new habits of thought. This is the most important thing you can spend your time on.

If you do not do this you have chosen to be only as rich as you are right now!

The Seven Day Mental Diet to the Right Use of the Will

1. For 7 days you must not allow yourself to dwell for a single moment on any kind of negative thought about money, poverty, affordability, or financial lack of any kind for yourself or anyone else.

2. You are to be consciously on guard for any negative thoughts about finances and should a thought come up you are not to dwell upon it. It is not the thoughts that come up that matter but only those that you choose to entertain or dwell upon.

3. For any negative thought given to you by another – you are to immediately dismiss it from your mind by affirming riches, wealth, and abundance. For Example: Your friend begins to talk about how he cannot afford a vacation this year. Do not try to shut him up or tell him that he is instrumental in producing his own situation. Let him talk and do not accept what he says and your mental diet will not be affected.

4. Nothing said or done by anyone else can take you off your diet only your reaction to the other person's conduct can do that.

5. Keep your "Mental Diet" a secret. Do not dissipate your energy by talking about it with others.

6. Read this Chapter three times a day for seven days.

Write the following thought on a small card and read it in the morning and the evening to internalize your "Mental Diet."

I will use my will to control my thoughts about money and getting rich.

As a result of your new learnings list the actions or goals will you are going to accomplish, so that you too can become rich by doing things "in a certain way"

1. I will control my thoughts about money + getting rich

2. I am free to travel all over the country, Europe, Asia, USA, Australia + South America, doing OM's in comfort staying in 5 * resorts + flying business class

3. I am free to live in a beautiful home with quality fixtures + fittings + a seaview + a sauna, in a nice area with lovely neighbours surrounded by quiet.

4. I am free to have thriving businesses with loyal clients/customers, quality products/ events, trustworthy talented staff/collaborators where I earn/generate millions of pounds per year.

5. I am free to buy clothes from Vivienne Westwood, Reiss + all nice places, go to events with wealthy people, mix with the celebrities + feel at home - I am refined, calm + strong.

6. I am free to have a wonderful global reputation, + be invited to participate in the most exclusive events + experiences around the world. I am free to be generous with my family + friends - help them financially + give them gifts.

Chapter Ten - Further Use Of The Will

You cannot retain a true and clear vision of wealth if you are constantly turning your attention to opposing pictures, whether they be external or imaginary.

Do not tell of your past troubles of a financial nature, if you have had them; do not think of them at all. Do not tell of the poverty of your parents, or the hardships of your early life; to do any of these things is to mentally class yourself with the poor for the time being, and it will certainly check the movement of things in your direction.

"Let the dead bury their dead," as Jesus said.

Put poverty and all things that pertain to poverty completely behind you.

You have accepted a certain theory of the universe as being correct, and are resting all your hopes of happiness on its being correct; and what can you gain by giving heed to conflicting theories?

Do not read religious books which tell you that the world is soon coming to an end; and do not read the writings of muck-rakers and pessimistic philosophers who tell you that it is going to the devil.

The world is not going to the devil; it is going to God.

It is a wonderful Becoming.

True, there may be a good many things in existing conditions which are disagreeable; but what is the use of studying them when they are certainly passing away, and when the study of them only tends to check their passing and keep them with us? Why give time and attention to things which are being removed by evolutionary growth, when you can hasten their removal only by promoting the evolutionary growth as far as your part of it goes?

No matter how horrible in seeming may be the conditions in certain countries, sections, or places, you waste your time and destroy your own chances by considering them.

You should interest yourself in the world's becoming rich.

Think of the riches the world is coming into, instead of the poverty it is growing out of; and bear in mind that the only way in which you can assist the world in growing rich is by growing rich yourself through the creative method—not the competitive one.

Give your attention wholly to riches; ignore poverty.

Whenever you think or speak of those who are poor, think and speak of them as those who are becoming rich, as those who are to be congratulated rather than pitied. Then they and others will catch the inspiration, and begin to search for the way out.

Because I say that you are to give your whole time and mind and thought to riches, it does not follow that you are to be sordid or mean.

To become really rich is the noblest aim you can have in life, for it includes everything else.

On the competitive plane, the struggle to get rich is a Godless scramble for power over other men, but when we come into the creative mind, all this is changed.

All that is possible in the way of greatness and soul unfoldment, of service and lofty endeavor, comes by way of getting rich; all is made possible by the use of things.

If you lack for physical health, you will find that the attainment of it is conditional on your getting rich.

Only those who are emancipated from financial worry, and who have the means to live a care-free existence and follow hygienic practices, can have and retain health.

Moral and spiritual greatness is possible only to those who are above the competitive battle for existence; and only those who are becoming rich on the plane of creative thought are free from the degrading influences of competition. If your heart is set on domestic happiness, remember that love flourishes best where there is refinement, a high level of thought, and freedom from corrupting influences; and these are to be found only where riches are attained by the exercise of creative thought, without strife or rivalry.

You can aim at nothing so great or noble, I repeat, as to become rich; and you must fix your attention upon your mental picture of riches, to the exclusion of all that may tend to dim or obscure the vision.

You must learn to see the underlying TRUTH in all things; you must see beneath all seemingly wrong conditions the Great One Life ever moving forward toward fuller expression and more complete happiness.

It is the truth that there is no such thing as poverty, that there is only wealth.

Some people remain in poverty because they are ignorant of the fact that there is wealth for them; and these can best be taught by showing them the way to affluence in your own person and practice.

Others are poor because, while they feel that there is a way out, they are too intellectually indolent to put forth the mental effort necessary to find that way and travel it; and for these the very best thing you can do is to arouse their desire by showing them the happiness that comes from being rightly rich.

Others still are poor because, while they have some notion of science, they have become so swamped and lost in the maze of metaphysical and occult theories that they do not know which road to take. They try a mixture of many systems and fail in all. For these, again, the very best thing to do is to show the right way in your own person and practice; an ounce of doing things is worth a pound of theorizing.

The very best thing you can do for the whole world is to make the most of yourself.

You can serve God and man in no more effective way than by getting rich; that is, if you get rich by the creative method, and not by the competitive one.

Another thing. We assert that this book gives in detail the principles of the science of getting rich; and if that is true, you do not need to read any other book upon the subject. This may sound narrow and egotistical, but consider: there is no more scientific method of computation in mathematics than by addition, subtraction, multiplication, and division; no other method is possible. There can be but one shortest distance between two points. There is only one way to think scientifically, and that is to think in the way that leads by the most direct and simple route to the goal. No man has yet formulated a briefer or less complex "system" than the one set forth herein; it has been stripped of all non-essentials. When you commence on this, lay all others aside; put them out of your mind altogether.

Read this book every day; keep it with you; commit it to memory, and do not think about other "systems" and theories. If you do, you will begin to have doubts, and to be uncertain and wavering in your thought, and then you will begin to make failures.

After you have made good and become rich, you may study other systems as much as you please, but until you are quite sure that you have gained what you want, do not read anything on this line but this book, unless it be the authors mentioned in the Preface.

And read only the most optimistic comments on the world's news; those in harmony with your picture.

Also, postpone your investigations into the occult. Do not dabble in Theosophy, Spiritualism, or kindred studies. It is very likely that the dead still live, and are near; but if they are, let them alone; mind your own business.

Wherever the spirits of the dead may be, they have their own work to do, and their own problems to solve, and we have no right to interfere with them. We cannot help them, and it is very doubtful whether they can help us, or whether we have any right to trespass upon their time if they can. Let the dead and the hereafter alone, and solve your own problem; get rich. If you begin to mix with the occult, you will start mental cross-currents which will surely bring your hopes to shipwreck. Now, this and the preceding chapters have brought us to the following statement of basic facts:

There is a thinking stuff from which all things are made, and which, in its original state, permeates, penetrates and fills the interspaces of the Universe.

A thought, in this substance, produces the thing that is imagined by the thought.

Man can form things in his thoughts and, by impressing his thought upon formless substance, can cause the thing he thinks about to be created.

In order to do this, man must pass from the competitive to the creative mind: he must form a clear mental picture of the things he wants, and hold this picture in his thoughts with the fixed PURPOSE to get what he wants, and the unwavering FAITH that he does get what he wants, closing his mind against all that may tend to shake his purpose, dim his vision, or quench his faith.

And in addition to all this, we shall now see that he must live and act in a Certain Way.

Chapter Ten - Taking Action

Understanding Chapter Ten

Further Use of the Will

1.   What happens when you relive, talk about and think about past financial failures?

It will stop me getting rich.

2.   What is the best thing you can do for the world?

Make the best of myself.

"All the power you can ever use now exists and awaits your intelligent mastery." – Dr. Edward Kramer.

"Whatever you permit yourself to think what persons, things, conditions or circumstances may suggest, you are not thinking what you yourself want to think. You are following borrowed desires instead of your own desires. Therefore, you will drift into strange thinking, thinking that is entirely different from what you had planned and that may be directly opposed to your present purpose, need or ambition."
– Christian D. Larson

Chapter Ten Learnings

The most Important principles, concepts and thoughts that I have learned from this Chapter are:

1. _Stoop going on about my past hardships_

2. _Stop talking about how my parents lost their house_

3. _Stop talking about how my mum worked hard_

4. _Stop thinking about my parents mortgage_

5. _Stop thinking about how my dad lost the house_

6. Stop thinking about how my dad contributed hardly anything

7. Stop thinking about how my dad took £5 from my uni savings when I was 4.

8. Stop thinking about my dad's 'get rich quick' schemes.

Chapter Ten Learnings

The two most Important principles, concepts and thoughts that I have learned from this Chapter and will use in my life are:

Principle One:

The best thing I can for the world is make the best for myself.

Principle Two:

There is no such thing as poverty only wealth

"To become a master mind you must think what you want to think, no matter what your surroundings may suggest. And you must continue to think what you want to think until each particular purpose is carried out and every desired ideal is realized. Make it a point to desire what you want to desire and impress that desire so deeply upon consciousness that it cannot possibly be disturbed by such foreign desires that the environment may suggest. Then continue to express that desire in all thought and action until you get what you want." – Christian D. Larson.

Putting the Science of Getting Rich Principles to Work

Recognize: Principle One I recognize in this Chapter is:

The best thing I can do for the world
is to make the best of myself.

Relate: What does this mean to me? What will this principle do for me?

I will earn £100,000 at least per year.
I will have a nice house ~~were~~ with luxury
comfortable furnishings & a seaview.
I will have @ investments + savings
that are well-managed + generate
a very good monthly passive income.

Assimilate: How can I use the principles to achieve my goals/riches?

I will always be open to new +
exciting opportunities & know I can
be successful. My father's failure
is not my failure.

Apply: How am I going to use it? Action steps. Do It Now!

I am going to phone the bank
+ ask how much equity I can borrow
Then ask Steve about the best property
to get. I think my criteria is to
buy 3 properties from the council
that are safe tenants & I get a regular
income but I also get the asset.
Monday I am starting.

Putting the Science of Getting Rich Principles to Work

Recognize: Principle Two I recognize in this Chapter is:

There is no such thing as poverty only wealth.

Relate: What does this mean to me? What will this principle do for me?

Everyone can benefit from these teachings. I can learn how to get rich just as I learnt to do all these other amazing things that have changed my life. By being rich I can be a good example to all

Assimilate: How can I use the principles to achieve my goals/riches?

I can embed this in my psyche. We live in a world governed by money + this is just a concept. I can be part of creating money for myself to benefit all.

Apply: How am I going to use it? Action steps. Do It Now!

I am going to research a wonderful centre for humanity.

Guard Your Thoughts

1.   Write in the space below any thoughts that still come into your mind that you know in your heart of hearts will not help you get rich. (Make a copy of this page on use this process to guard you thoughts as needed.)

Example: I don't have the capital to start a business of my own.

I don't have the capital to start a business
That Being a landlady can be difficult to manage
The market might turn
I don't have the skills or expertise
The bank might not lend me the money
I don't have regular income.

2.   Now take each of these thoughts, one at a time, and in the space below write out what the exact opposite (positive) thought must be – using the thoughts and principles of The Science of Getting Rich.

Example: As I create my business all the capital that I need will be made available to me in ways that have not yet been determined.

All the capital will come to me to set up my business.
I will have all the help + guidance I need
to manage my properties
The market always goes up in S.E.
I can learn the skills + expertise
I will generate a regular income.

3.   Write out each of the above statements on 3 x 5 cards. Assimilate these new beliefs any by reading them several times a day. Contemplate the new beliefs in light of The Science of Getting Rich. By doing so you will replace the old worries, doubts and fears with truth and understanding.

Continue to Use

The Seven Day

Mental Diet

for the Right

Use of Will

For Another Week

As a result of your new learnings list the actions or goals will you are going to accomplish, so that you too can become rich by doing things "in a certain way"

1. Start looking at properties

2. Find out how much I can borrow

3. Meet with Steve regularly

4. Read more about property

5. Let go of fears of property ownership

6. Forget being mortage-free + INVEST Now!

~~£1615~~

£150,000

£850 per month

2 Bed

Brighton

nice kitchen.

less than 20 mins
from Centre.

$$\begin{array}{r} 850 \times \\ 10 \\ \hline 8500 \end{array}$$

8500

150,000

Chapter Eleven - Acting In A Certain Way

Thought is the creative power, or the impelling force which causes the creative power to act; thinking in a Certain Way will bring riches to you, but you must not rely upon thought alone, paying no attention to personal action. That is the rock upon which many otherwise scientific metaphysical thinkers meet shipwreck—the failure to connect thought with personal action.

We have not yet reached the stage of development, even supposing such a stage to be possible, in which man can create directly from Formless Substance without nature's processes or the work of human hands; man must not only think, but his personal action must supplement his thought.

By thought you can cause the gold in the hearts of the mountains to be impelled toward you, but it will not mine itself, refine itself, coin itself into, double eagles, and come rolling along the roads seeking its way into your pocket.

Under the impelling power of the Supreme Spirit, men's affairs will be so ordered that some one will be led to mine the gold for you; other men's business transactions will be so directed that the gold will be brought toward you, and you must so arrange your own business affairs that you may be able to receive it when it comes to you. Your thought makes all things, animate and inanimate, work to bring you what you want; but your personal activity must be such that you can rightly receive what you want when it reaches you. You are not to take it as charity, nor to steal it; you must give every man more in use value than he gives you in cash value.

The scientific use of thought consists in forming a clear and distinct mental image of what you want; in holding fast to the purpose to get what you want, and in realizing with grateful faith that you do get what you want.

Do not try to "project" your thought in any mysterious or occult way, with the idea of having it go out and do things for you; that is wasted effort, and will weaken your power to think with sanity.

The action of thought in getting rich is fully explained in the preceding chapters; your faith and purpose positively impress your vision upon Formless Substance, which has THE SAME DESIRE FOR MORE LIFE THAT YOU HAVE; and this vision, received from you, sets all the creative forces at work IN AND THROUGH THEIR REGULAR CHANNELS OF ACTION, but directed toward you.

It is not your part to guide or supervise the creative process; all you have to do with that is to retain your vision, stick to your purpose, and maintain your faith and gratitude.

But you must act in a Certain Way, so that you can appropriate what is yours when it comes to you; so that you can meet the things you have in your picture, and put them in their proper places as they arrive.

You can readily see the truth of this. When things reach you, they will be in the hands of other men, who will ask an equivalent for them.

And you can only get what is yours by giving the other man what is his.

Your pocketbook is not going to be transformed into a Fortunatus purse, which shall be always full of money without effort on your part.

This is the crucial point in the science of getting rich; right here, where thought and personal action must be combined. There are very many people who, consciously or unconsciously, set the creative forces in action by the strength and persistence of their desires, but who remain poor because they do not provide for the reception of the thing they want when it comes.

By thought, the thing you want is brought to you; by action you receive it.

Whatever your action is to be, it is evident that you must act NOW. You cannot act in the past, and it is essential to the clearness of your mental vision that you dismiss the past from your mind. You cannot act in the future for the future is not here yet. And you cannot tell how you will want to act in any future contingency until that contingency has arrived.

Because you are not in the right business, or the right environment now, do not think that you must postpone action until you get into the right business or environment. And do not spend time in the present taking thought as to the best course in possible future emergencies; have faith in your ability to meet any emergency when it arrives.

If you act in the present with your mind on the future, your present action will be with a divided mind, and will not be effective.

Put your whole mind into present action.

Do not give your creative impulse to Original Substance, and then sit down and wait for results; if you do, you will never get them. Act now. There is never any time but now, and there never will be any time but now. If you are ever to begin to make ready for the reception of what you want, you must begin now.

And your action, whatever it is, must most likely be in your present business or employment, and must be upon the persons and things in your present environment.

You cannot act where you are not; you cannot act where you have been, and you cannot act where you are going to be; you can only act where you are.

Do not bother as to whether yesterday's work was well done or ill done; do to-day's work well.

Do not try to do to-morrow's work now; there will be plenty of time to do that when you get to it.

Do not try, by occult or mystical means, to act on people or things that are out of your reach.

Do not wait for a change of environment before you act; get a change of environment by action.

You can so act upon the environment in which you are now, as to cause yourself to be transferred to a better environment.

Hold with faith and purpose the vision of yourself in the better environment, but act upon your present environment with all your heart, and with all your strength, and with all your mind.

Do not spend any time in daydreaming or castle building; hold to the one vision of what you want, and act NOW.

Do not cast about seeking some new thing to do, or some strange, unusual, or remarkable action to perform as a first step toward getting rich. It is probable that your actions, at least for some time to come, will be those you have been performing for some time past; but you are to begin now to perform these actions in the Certain Way, which will surely make you rich.

If you are engaged in some business, and feel that it is not the right one for you, do not wait until you get into the right business before you begin to act.

Do not feel discouraged, or sit down and lament because you are misplaced. No man was ever so misplaced but that he could find the right place, and no man ever became so involved in the wrong business but that he could get into the right business.

Hold the vision of yourself in the right business, with the purpose to get into it, and the faith that you will get into it, and are getting into it; but ACT in your present business. Use your present business as the means of getting a better one, and use your present environment as the means of getting into a better one. Your vision of the right business, if held with faith and purpose, will cause the Supreme to move the right business toward you; your action, if performed in the Certain Way, will cause you to move toward the business.

If you are an employee, or wage earner, and feel that you must change places in order to get what you want, do not "project" your thought into space and rely upon it to get you another job. It will probably fail to do so.

Hold the vision of yourself in the job you want, while you ACT with faith and purpose on the job you have, and you will certainly get the job you want.

Your vision and faith will set the creative force in motion to bring it toward you, and your action will cause the forces in your own environment to move you toward the place you want. In closing this chapter, we will add another statement to our syllabus:

There is a thinking stuff from which all things are made, and which, in its original state, permeates, penetrates, and fills the interspaces of the universe.

A thought, in this substance, produces the thing that is imaged by the thought.

Man can form things in his thought, and, by impressing his thoughts upon formless substance, can cause the thing he thinks about to be created.

In order to do this, man must pass from the competitive to the creative mind, he must form a clear mental picture of the things he wants, and hold this picture in his thoughts with the fixed PURPOSE to get what he wants, and the unwavering FAITH that he does get what he wants, closing his mind to all that may tend to shake his purpose, dim his vision, or quench his faith.

That he may receive what he wants when it comes, man must act NOW upon the people and things in his present environment.

Chapter Eleven - Taking Action
Understanding Chapter Eleven
Acting in the Certain Way

1. Complete this thought, "The scientific use of thought consists of......"

    Forming a clear + distinct mental image, in holding fast to what you want and realizing inthe grateful faith when you do get what you want.

2. What must we do in addition to creative thinking?

    We must act now!

3. How does action connect with thought?

    Put your whole mind into present action.

4. Should you stop your current action? If not, why not?

    No you can only start from where you are right now, not where you were yesterday or tomorrow.

"Just as today is a result of past thinking, so the future will be a result of what is built today. Therefore you do things in a certain way today and KNOW with mathematical certainty what the result will be."

163

Chapter Eleven Learnings

The most Important principles, concepts and thoughts that I have learned from this Chapter are:

1. Put your whole mind into the present action

2. Do not wait for results

3. Act now!

4. Do it in your present business or environment

5. Do your best work now

6.   Work in the present

7.   Do not lament

8.   Hold a vision of yourself in the right business.

Chapter Eleven Learnings

The two most Important principles, concepts and thoughts that I have learned from this Chapter and will use in my life are:

Principle One:

Focus your mind on the present

Principle Two:

Take action now

"The first step to success lies right where you are and what you are currently doing."

"If your mind is on the past – you cannot act.
If your mind is on the future – you cannot act.
You can only act now, right here, right now in the present."

Putting the Science of Getting Rich Principles to Work

Recognize: Principle One I recognize in this Chapter is:

Focus your mind on the present

Relate: What does this mean to me? What will this principle do for me?

Start with where I am now - my current sources of income, savings + investments.

Assimilate: How can I use the principles to achieve my goals/riches?

Look into buying a property in Brighton + good tenants - £850 per month at least

Apply: How am I going to use it? Action steps. Do It Now!

Start researching
Call bank on Monday - see how much I can borrow
Best buy to let interest only rates
Book some viewings
DO IT NOW

Putting the Science of Getting Rich Principles to Work

Recognize: Principle Two I recognize in this Chapter is:

Take action now

Relate: What does this mean to me? What will this principle do for me?

No need to keep dwelling on the past failures, start new to make changes + reap the rewards.

Assimilate: How can I use the principles to achieve my goals/riches?

I can start looking at all different flats + houses, repossessions with highest rental yield, to flats for sale in Brighton.

Apply: How am I going to use it? Action steps. Do It Now!

Start researching
Get on with it!
Talk to Estate agents
Talk to lenders
Talk to Steve.

Taking Action

In order to achieve my desires that I have Treasure Mapped. Here are the actions that I am going to take within the next 48 hours in order that I may receive my own good.

1. _Phone Bank - see how much I can get_

2. _Start viewing flats in Central Brighton_

3. _Start looking at mortgage rates_

4. _Start talking to Estate agents_

5. _Talk to Steve_

Continue to review and revise your "Treasure Map" of your most important desire.

As a result of your new learnings list the actions or goals will you are going to accomplish, so that you too can become rich by doing things "in a certain way"

1. Be in the present

2. Forget the past

3. Do the research

4. Start where I am now

5. Follow my gut - ask for help

6. Be grateful!

172

Chapter Twelve - Efficient Action

You must use your thought as directed in previous chapters, and begin to do what you can do where you are; and you must do ALL that you can do where you are.

You can advance only by being larger than your present place; and no man is larger than his present place who leaves undone any of the work pertaining to that place.

The world is advanced only by those who more than fill their present places.

If no man quite filled his present place, you can see that there must be a going backward in everything. Those who do not quite fill their present places are a dead weight upon society, government, commerce, and industry; they must be carried along by others at a great expense. The progress of the world is retarded only by those who do not fill the places they are holding; they belong to a former age and a lower stage or plane of life, and their tendency is toward degeneration. No society could advance if every man was smaller than his place; social evolution is guided by the law of physical and mental evolution. In the animal world, evolution is caused by excess of life.

When an organism has more life than can be expressed in the functions of its own plane, it develops the organs of a higher plane, and a new species is originated.

There never would have been new species had there not been organisms which more than filled their places. The law is exactly the same for you; your getting rich depends upon your applying this principle to your own affairs.

Every day is either a successful day or a day of failure; and it is the successful days which get you what you want. If every day is a failure, you can never get rich; while if every day is a success, you cannot fail to get rich.

If there is something that may be done today, and you do not do it, you have failed in so far as that thing is concerned, and the consequences may be more disastrous than you imagine.

You cannot foresee the results of even the most trivial act; you do not know the workings of all the forces that have been set moving in your behalf. Much may be depending on your doing some simple act; it may be the very thing which is to open the door of opportunity to very great possibilities. You can never know all the combinations which Supreme Intelligence is making for you in the world of things and of human affairs; your neglect or failure to do some small thing may cause a long delay in getting what you want.

Do, everyday, ALL that can be done that day.

There is, however, a limitation or qualification of the above that you must take into account.

You are not to overwork, nor to rush blindly into your business in the effort to do the greatest possible number of things in the shortest possible time.

You are not to try to do tomorrow's work today, nor to do a week's work in a day.

It is really not the number of things you do, but the EFFICIENCY of each separate action that counts

Every act is, in itself, either a success or a failure.

Every act is, in itself, either effective or inefficient.

Every inefficient act is a failure, and if you spend your life in doing inefficient acts, your whole life will be a failure.

The more things you do, the worse for you, if all your acts are inefficient ones.

On the other hand, every efficient act is a success in itself, and if every act of your life is an efficient one, your whole life MUST be a success.

The cause of failure is doing too many things in an inefficient manner and not doing enough things in an efficient manner.

You will see that it is a self-evident proposition that if you do not do any inefficient acts, and do a sufficient number of efficient acts, you will become rich. If, now, it is possible for you to make each act an efficient one, you see again that the getting of riches is reduced to an exact science, like mathematics.

The matter turns, then, on the question whether you can make each separate act a success in itself. And this you can certainly do.

You can make each act a success, because All Power is working with you, and All Power cannot fail.

Power is at your service, and to make each act efficient you have only to put power into it.

Every action is either strong or weak; and when every one is strong, you are acting in the Certain Way which will make you rich.

Every act can be made strong and efficient by holding your vision while you are doing it, and putting the whole power of your FAITH and PURPOSE into it.

It is at this point that the people fail who separate mental power from personal action. They use the power of mind in one place and at one time, and they act in another place and at another time. So their acts are not successful in themselves; too many of them are inefficient. But if ALL Power goes into every act, no matter how commonplace, every act will be a success in itself; and as in the nature of things every success opens the way to other successes, your progress toward what you want, and the progress of what you want toward you, will become increasingly rapid.

Remember that successful action is cumulative in its results. Since the desire for more life is inherent in all things, when a man begins to move toward larger life more things attach themselves to him, and the influence of his desire is multiplied.

Do, every day, all that you can do that day, and do each act in an efficient manner.

In saying that you must hold your vision while you are doing each act, however trivial or commonplace, I do not mean to say that it is necessary at all times to see the vision distinctly to its smallest details. It should be the work of your leisure hours to use your imagination on the details of your vision, and to contemplate them until they are firmly fixed upon your memory

If you wish speedy results, spend practically all your spare time in this practice.

By continuous contemplation you will get the picture of what you want, even to the smallest details, so firmly fixed upon your mind, and so completely transferred to the mind of Formless Substance, that in your working hours you need only to mentally refer to the picture to stimulate your faith and purpose, and cause your best effort to be put forth. Contemplate your picture in your leisure hours until your consciousness is so full of it that you can grasp it instantly. You will become so enthused with its bright promises that the mere thought of it will call forth the strongest energies of your whole being.

Let us again repeat our syllabus, and by slightly changing the closing statements bring it to the point we have now reached.

There is a thinking stuff from which all things are made, and which, in its original state, permeates, penetrates, and fills *the interspaces of the universe.*

A thought, in this substance, produces the thing that is imagined by the thought.

Man can form things in his thought, and, by impressing his thought upon formless substance, can cause the thing he thinks about to be created.

In order to do this, man must pass from the competitive to the creative mind, he must form a clear mental picture of the things he wants, and do, with faith and purpose, all that can be done each day, doing each separate thing in an efficient manner.

Chapter Twelve - Taking Action
Understanding Chapter Twelve
Efficient Action

1. How may you advance?

    By doing what needs to be done today, efficiently
    I must fill my present place

2. Why must you do every day?

    Do what needs to be done

3. What is the cause of failure?

    Every ineffective act is a failure

4. How do you make every act strong and efficient?

    Do not do any in
    Hold your vision + put the whole
    FAITH + POWER into it.

5. What must you do each day?

    Do all you can do that day
    in an effective manner.

Chapter Twelve Learnings

The most Important principles, concepts and thoughts that I have learned from this Chapter are:

1. Do all you can do every day in the most effictive manner

2. Know you cannot fail because each day hold your vision + put all y

3. Put all your faith + power into your vision + you cannot fail

4. Spend your spare time holding your vision

5. The this See the vision clearly in the most minute details

6. You must do what needs to be done each day

7. Do each thing in the most efficient many manner

8. Don't overwork.

Chapter Twelve Learnings

The two most Important principles, concepts and thoughts that I have learned from this Chapter and will use in my life are:

Principle One:

Hold a clear vision every day of your goal

Principle Two:

Do each thing every day in the most effective way

"Every act you take either moves you forward towards your goals or in the opposite direction."

"The ancestor of every action is a thought." - Emerson

Putting the Science of Getting Rich Principles to Work

Recognize: Principle One I recognize in this Chapter is:

Hold a clear vision

Relate: What does this mean to me? What will this principle do for me?

Work out what it means to be rich

How will I know I am rich

When I need to find out what I really want

Assimilate: How can I use the principles to achieve my goals/riches?

I can write a clear list with
a clear deadline of what I want

Apply: How am I going to use it? Action steps. Do It Now!

I'm going to write a list of
my dream portfolio:
- stocks + investments
- property
- passive income
- salary / paid work
- reiki / deeksha / onus.

Putting the Science of Getting Rich Principles to Work

Recognize: Principle Two I recognize in this Chapter is:

Do what needs to be done each day

Relate: What does this mean to me? What will this principle do for me?

Act efficiently each day

Assimilate: How can I use the principles to achieve my goals/riches?

By doing research to + learning
for myself, how to do my accounts,
working out property renting,
learning how stocks work, I can
learn how to be rich

Apply: How am I going to use it? Action steps. Do It Now!

I am going to do my homework
Write down my goals
Work out what makes me passionate
What is real wealth?
How can Do A Robbin's Wealth Mastery course.
Listen to Rhana's advice.

Efficient Action

1. Are your actions efficient now? Yes ~~or No~~

2. If Yes. Write down 3 ways that you may improve the efficiency of your actions. How may you more than fill your current place?

   ① Plan my day better — relax every day — get out + get fresh air — exercise every day

   ② Get up earlier

   ③ Don't get distracted by FB / Twitter too much

3. If No. Write down how you intend to fill your current place. Include action steps and dates that you will complete these action steps.

Creating a Successful Life

It is really not the number of things you do, but the EFFICIENCY of each separate action that counts.

Every act is, in itself, either effective or inefficient.

Every inefficient act is a failure, and if you spend your life in doing inefficient acts, your whole life will be a failure.

The more things you do, the worse for you, if all your acts are inefficient ones.

On the other hand, every efficient act is a success in itself, and if every act of your life is an efficient one, your whole life MUST be a success.

The cause of failure is doing too many things in an inefficient manner and not doing enough things in an efficient manner.

You will see that it is a self-evident proposition that if you do not do any inefficient acts, and do a sufficient number of efficient acts, you will become rich. If, now, it is possible for you to make each act an efficient one, you see again that the getting of riches is reduced to an exact science, like mathematics.

I am going to multiple by TEN my efforts to do more efficient acts. I will do that in these ways.

1. Get more digital work by ensuring work is done efficiently.

2. Plan digital work better so work is delivered in plenty of time to test + fix bugs.

3. I will make sure I check ~~the~~ developers work — spelling + designs v build before it goes to the client.

4. I will go to hot yoga when I say I will go —

5. I will drink water every hour + rest when it's time to rest

6. I will make sure developer gets the laptop + installs it + checks it on Friday, + I will be present when I do this.

7. I will get more reiki clients regularly coming for treatments

8. I will make sure people pay donations properly for deeksha

9. I will get more people to reiki courses to pay full price.

As a result of your new learnings list the actions or goals will you are going to accomplish, so that you too can become rich by doing things "in a certain way"

1. Work out new dates for reiki courses + add them to the site - including Reiki Master level

2. I will work out dates for Dublin, Glasgow, Amsterdam but make sure it's for fun not clashing with reiki courses.

3. I will update reiki site

4. I will get more PM work at £350 - £555 day rate

5. I will work with my own team of writers, developers + designers + charge accurately with contingency + huge margin

6. I will brush up my strategy, business + accounting skills.

Chapter Thirteen - Getting Into The Right Business

Success, in any particular business, depends for one thing upon your possessing in a well-developed state the faculties required in that business.

Without good musical faculty no one can succeed as a teacher of music; without well-developed mechanical faculties no one can achieve great success in any of the mechanical trades; without tact and the commercial faculties no one can succeed in mercantile pursuits. But to possess in a well-developed state the faculties required in your particular vocation does not insure getting rich. There are musicians who have remarkable talent, and who yet remain poor; there are blacksmiths, carpenters, and so on who have excellent mechanical ability but who do not get rich; and there are merchants with good faculties for dealing with men who nevertheless fail.

The different faculties are tools; it is essential to have good tools, but it is also essential that the tools should be used in the Right Way. One man can take a sharp saw, a square, a good plane, and so on, and build a handsome article of furniture; another man can take the same tools and set to work to duplicate the article, but his production will be a botch. He does not know how to use good tools in a successful way.

The various faculties of your mind are the tools with which you must do the work which is to make you rich; it will be easier for you to succeed if you get into a business for which you are well equipped with mental tools.

Generally speaking, you will do best in that business which will use your strongest faculties; the one for which you are naturally "best fitted." But there are limitations to this statement, also. No man should regard his vocation as being irrevocably fixed by the tendencies with which he was born.

You can get rich in ANY business, for if you have not the right talent for it you can develop that talent; it merely means that you will have to make your tools as you go along, instead of confining yourself to the use of those with which you were born. It will be EASIER for you to succeed in a vocation for which you already have talents in a well-developed state, but you CAN succeed in any vocation, for you can develop any rudimentary talents of which you have not at least the rudiment.

You will get rich most easily in point of effort, if you do that for which you are best fitted; but you will get rich most satisfactorily if you do that which you WANT to do.

Doing what you want to do is life; and there is no real satisfaction in living if we are compelled to be forever doing something which we do not like to do, and can never do what we want to do. And it is certain that you can do what you want to do; the desire to do it is proof that you have within you the power which can do it.

Desire is a manifestation of power.

The desire to play music is the power which can play music seeking expression and development; the desire to invent mechanical devices is the mechanical talent seeking expression and development.

Where there is no power, either developed or undeveloped, to do a thing, there is never any desire to do that thing; and where there is strong desire to do a thing, it is certain proof that the power to do it is strong, and only requires to be developed and applied in the Right Way.

All things else being equal, it is best to select the business for which you have the best developed talent, but if you have a strong desire to engage in any particular line of work, you should select that work as the ultimate end at which you aim.

You can do what you want to do, and it is your right and privilege to follow the business or avocation which will be most congenial and pleasant.

You are not obliged to do what you do not like to do, and should not do it except as a means to bring you to the doing of the thing you want to do.

If there are past mistakes whose consequences have placed you in an undesirable business or environment, you may be obliged for some time to do what you do not like to do, but you can make the doing of it pleasant by knowing that it is making it possible for you to come to the doing of what you want to do.

If you feel that you are not in the right vocation, do not act too hastily in tying to get into another one. The best way, generally, to change business or environment is by growth.

Do not be afraid to make a sudden and radical change if the opportunity is presented, and you feel after careful consideration that it is the right opportunity; but never take sudden or radical action when you are in doubt as to the wisdom of doing so.

There is never any hurry on the creative plane; and there is no lack of opportunity.

When you get out of the competitive mind you will understand that you never need to act hastily. No one else is going to beat you to the thing you want to do; there is enough for all. If one place is taken, another and a better one will be opened for you a little farther on; there is plenty of time. When you are in doubt, wait. Fall back on the contemplation of your vision, and increase your faith and purpose; and by all means, in times of doubt and indecision, cultivate gratitude.

A day or two spent in contemplating the vision of what you want, and in earnest thanksgiving that you are getting it, will bring your mind into such close relationship with the Supreme that you will make no mistake when you do act.

There is a mind which knows all there is to know; and you can come into close unity with this mind by faith and the purpose to advance in life, if you have deep gratitude.

Mistakes come from acting hastily, or from acting in fear or doubt, or in forgetfulness of the Right Motive, which is more life to all, and less to none.

As you go on in the Certain Way, opportunities will come to you in increasing numbers; and you will need to be very steady in your faith and purpose, and to keep in close touch with the All Mind by reverent gratitude.

Do all that you can do in a perfect manner every day, but do it without haste, worry, or fear. Go as fast as you can, but never hurry.

Remember that in the moment you begin to hurry you cease to be a creator and become a competitor; you drop back upon the old plane again.

Whenever you find yourself hurrying, call a halt; fix your attention on the mental image of the thing you want, and begin to give thanks that you are getting it. The exercise of GRATITUDE will never fail to strengthen your faith and renew your purpose.

Chapter Thirteen - Taking Action
Understanding Chapter Thirteen
Getting Into the Right Business

1. Why does success, in any particular business depend on your processing in a well-developed state the faculties required in that business?

    You need the right tools to do your business. A

2. In what way are faculties like tools?

    You need the right skills + aptitude + need to use them in the right way in order to be successful.

3. What is desire?

    Desire is the manifestation of Power

4. What does having a desire mean?

    The power wants to express itself through that medium

5. Why is there never any hurry on the creative plane?

    There is no lack, no competition. No-one is going to take away the opportunity.

Chapter Thirteen Learnings

The most Important principles, concepts and thoughts that I have learned from this Chapter are:

1. Success depends on me using + developing my skills + talents

2. There is no need to hurry on the creative plane

3. I need to use my skills + talents in the right way.

4. # Desire to do something is the expression of Power wanting to manifest.

5. Do work that you find most pleasant.

6. You don't have to do work you don't want to do

7. You will get rich doing the work that suits you best

8. I might have to spend a bit of time doing work I don't like until I get to do what I want to.

Chapter Thirteen Learnings

The two most Important principles, concepts and thoughts that I have learned from this Chapter and will use in my life are:

Principle One:

Do work that you like best

Principle Two:

Use the skills + talents you have already.

"All the money that comes into your life comes through other people."

"The destiny of every individual is determined by what they are and by what they are doing. And any individual is to be or do is determined by what they are living for, thinking for, or working for, be those objects great or small, superior or inferior.

– Christian D. Larson.

Putting the Science of Getting Rich Principles to Work

Recognize: Principle One I recognize in this Chapter is:

Do work that you like best

Relate: What does this mean to me? What will this principle do for me?

Working with people
Working in technology with cutting edge stuff
with designers + developers
Organising events
Healing people
Running courses I have lots of ski

Assimilate: How can I use the principles to achieve my goals/riches?

I can focus all my skills + talents
+ work out what I like + dislike

Apply: How am I going to use it? Action steps. Do It Now!

I can use Rhona's exercise today
x work out what I like + dislike
+ what I really want.

Putting the Science of Getting Rich Principles to Work

Recognize: Principle Two I recognize in this Chapter is:

Use the skills + talent that you have

Relate: What does this mean to me? What will this principle do for me?

I need to focus on the things I like doing + the things I am good at in order to create money.

Assimilate: How can I use the principles to achieve my goals/riches?

Instead of thinking about the How it is better to focus on WHAT I am good at + all the things I have already achieved.

Apply: How am I going to use it? Action steps. Do It Now!

Do the exercise
Research property buying
Look at some properties

BE CLEAR ON GOALS - Being Mortgage free is my TOP PRIORITY.

Getting In The Right Business

I am in the Business I want to be in!

1. What well developed faculties are required for you to be successful at this business?

    Understanding of the market, simple Maths: mortage + interest rates. Monthly yield. Landlady.

2. Which of these faculties are you skilled at right now?

    Organising, negotitiating, networking, marketing, people skills.

3. Which of these faculties are you NOT skilled at right now?

    Practical fixing things in house. Legal + conveyancing. Surveys.

4. Do you need to develop these faculties yourself or can you hire someone else who has them to work for you? I can hire someone to fix stuff + a lawyer.

5. What are your action steps to develop the faculties that you require for the business that you are in? How will you acquire each of these faculties?

Faculty	How I will acquire it.	Date I will have acquired it.
1. Understand market -	Chat to Steve -	by FRIDAY 1 Nov
2. Research housing in Brighton -	Internet	by Fri 1 Nov
3. Check out properties -		on Fri 1 Nov
4. Talk to bank -	by Fri 1 Nov.	

Getting In The Right Business

I am NOT in the Business I want to be in!

1. Write a clear and definite description of the business that you would like to be in.

   I would like to have a co-working space for people to rent out + a space I can hold events. I want to own outright flats + houses in Brighton + rent them out to people + gain a very good return when I sell ~~and make~~ as well as a ~~no~~ very good 12% monthly yield.

2. Use the "Treasure Map Process" from the previous chapter to impress upon Formless Substance the business that you desire.

3. Contemplate the vision of what you want, with earnest thanksgiving that you are getting it. Hold it in your mind with your will. Do all that you can do each day to move toward it. List here actions that you will take in the next seven days to move toward it.

   I will look at properties, research the market + look at ways to finance my flats. I will find a good lawyer in January. There is no need to hurry or rush into this process. There are better ways to finance my goals than mortgaging the house.
   MY TOP GOAL IS TO ~~R~~ BE MORTGAGE-FREE.

As a result of your new learnings list the actions or goals will you are going to accomplish, so that you too can become rich by doing things "in a certain way"

1. Research flats/houses
    Budget my spending to £100 per week.

2. Look at financing / conveyancing

3. know that I need help with legal aspects

4. know that I need help with fixing properties

5. know that finding property is stresful + buying + selling is stresful

6. Know that my TOP PRIORITY IS TO BE MORTGAGE - FREE.

Chapter Fourteen - The Impression Of Increase

Whether you change your vocation or not, your actions for the present must be those pertaining to the business in which you are now engaged.

You can get into the business you want by making constructive use of the business you are already established in; by doing your daily work in a Certain Way.

And in so far as your business consists in dealing with other men, whether personally or by letter, the key-thought of all your efforts must be to convey to their minds the impression of increase.

Increase is what all men and all women are seeking; it is the urge of the Formless Intelligence within them, seeking fuller expression.

The desire for increase is inherent in all nature; it is the fundamental impulse of the universe. All human activities are based on the desire for increase; people are seeking more food, more clothes, better shelter, more luxury, more beauty, more knowledge, more pleasure—increase in something, more life.

Every living thing is under that necessity for continuous advancement; where increase of life ceases, dissolution and death set in at once.

Man instinctively knows this, and hence he is forever seeking more. This law of perpetual increase is set forth by Jesus in the parable of the talents; only those who gain more retain more; from him who hath not shall be taken away even that which he hath.

The normal desire for increased wealth is not an evil or a reprehensible thing; it is simply the desire for more abundant life; it is aspiration.

And because it is the deepest instinct of their natures, all men and women are attracted to him who can give them more of the means of life.

In following the Certain Way as described in the foregoing pages, you are getting continuous increase for yourself, and you are giving it to all with whom you deal.

You are a creative center, from which increase is given off to all.

Be sure of this, and convey assurance of the fact to every man, woman, and child with whom you come in contact. No matter how small the transaction, even if it be only the selling of a stick of candy to a little child, put into it the thought of increase, and make sure that the customer is impressed with the thought.

Convey the impression of advancement with everything you do, so that all people shall receive the impression that you are an Advancing Man, and that you advance all who deal with you. Even to the people whom you meet in a social way, without any thought of business, and to whom you do not try to sell anything, give the thought of increase.

You can convey this impression by holding the unshakable faith that you, yourself, are in the Way of Increase; and by letting this faith inspire, fill, and permeate every action.

Do everything that you do in the firm conviction that you are an advancing personality, and that you are giving advancement to everybody.

Feel that you are getting rich, and that in so doing you are making others rich, and conferring benefits on all.

Do not boast or brag of your success, or talk about it unnecessarily; true faith is never boastful.

Wherever you find a boastful person, you find one who is secretly doubtful and afraid. Simply feel the faith, and let it work out in every transaction; let every act and tone and look express the quiet assurance that you are getting rich, that you are already rich. Words will not be necessary to communicate this feeling to others; they will feel the sense of increase when in your presence, and will be attracted to you again.

You must so impress others that they will feel that in associating with you they will get increase for themselves. See that you give them a use value greater than the cash value you are taking from them.

Take an honest pride in doing this, and let everybody know it, and you will have no lack of customers. People will go where they are given increase, and the Supreme, which desires increase in all, and which knows all, will move toward you men and women who have never heard of you. Your business will increase rapidly, and you will be surprised at the unexpected benefits which will come to you. You will be able from day to day to make larger combinations, secure greater advantages, and to go on into a more congenial vocation if you desire to do so.

But in doing all this, you must never lose sight of your vision of what you want, or your faith and purpose to get what you want.

Let me here give you another word of caution in regard to motives.

Beware of the insidious temptation to seek for power over other men.

Nothing is so pleasant to the unformed or partially developed mind as the exercise of power or domination over others. The desire to rule for selfish gratification has been the curse of the world. For countless ages kings and lords have drenched the earth with blood in their battles to extend their dominions; this not to seek more life for all, but to get more power for themselves.

Today, the main motive in the business and industrial world is the same; men marshal their armies of dollars, and lay waste the lives and hearts of millions in the same mad scramble for power over others. Commercial kings, like political kings, are inspired by the lust for power.

Jesus saw in this desire for mastery the moving impulse of that evil world He sought to overthrow. Read the twenty-third chapter of Matthew, and see how He pictures the lust of the Pharisees to be called "master," to sit in the high places, to domineer over others, and to lay burdens on the backs of the less fortunate; and note how He compares this lust for dominion with the brotherly seeking for the Common Good to which He calls His disciples.

Look out for the temptation to seek for authority, to become a "master," to be considered as one who is above the common herd, to impress others by lavish display, and so on.

The mind that seeks for mastery over others is the competitive mind, and the competitive mind is not the creative one. In order to master your environment and your destiny, it is not at all necessary that you should rule over your fellow men; and indeed, when you fall into the world's struggle for the high places, you begin to be conquered by fate and environment, and your getting rich becomes a matter of chance and speculation.

Beware of the competitive mind! No better statement of the principle of creative action can be formulated than the favorite declaration of the late "Golden Rule" Jones of Toledo: "What I want for myself, I want for everybody."

Chapter Fourteen - Taking Action
Understanding Chapter Fourteen
The Impression of Increase

1. Why do all people desire increase?

   It is the urge of the formlen substance to continually increase

2. How do you convey the impression of increase to all that you meet?

   By following a certain way - holding an unshareable faith in myself that I am already rich + succenful that I am already an ADVANCING PERSONALITY

3. Why are you not to boast and brag about your success?

   Because there is no need to, I don't need to be secretly fearful or doubtful.

4. What does the Science of Getting Rich call the "insidious temptation"?

   To seek power over men and women.

"The recognition and conception of new sources of wealth is the loftiest aspiration you can take into your heart, for it assumes and implies the furtherance of all noble aims."

– G. Behrend.

Chapter Fourteen Learnings

The most Important principles, concepts and thoughts that I have learned from this Chapter are:

1. Do not seek power over men.

2. Act like a successful rich person always

3. Do not boast

4. Beware of the competitive mind

5. Remember there is no scarcity

6. Convey the impression of advancement
    in everything you do

7. Feel I am getting rich

8. Never lose sight of the vision
    of what you want

Chapter Fourteen Learnings

The two most Important principles, concepts and thoughts that I have learned from this Chapter and will use in my life are:

Principle One:

Feel + know I am getting rich

Principle Two:

Beware LORDING IT OVER OTHERS

"Thoughts engenders thought. Place one idea upon paper, another will follow it and still another, until you have written a page. You cannot fathom your mind. It is a well of thought which has no bottom. The more you draw from it, the more clear and fruitful it will be. If you neglect to think yourself, and use other people's thoughts, giving them utterances only, you will never know what you are capable of." – G.A. Sala.

Putting the Science of Getting Rich Principles to Work

Recognize: Principle One I recognize in this Chapter is:

Feel + Know I am getting rich

Relate: What does this mean to me? What will this principle do for me?

Keep getting more + more specific about what I want

Assimilate: How can I use the principles to achieve my goals/riches?

Hold a clear vision
keep a refining + getting clarity
know that I ~~can~~ am already
financially free + financially
independent

Apply: How am I going to use it? Action steps. Do It Now!

Keep doing my homework + look at
my fears + look for my dream home
knowing that it is coming.

Putting the Science of Getting Rich Principles to Work

Recognize: Principle Two I recognize in this Chapter is:

Do not seek to have power over others

Relate: What does this mean to me? What will this principle do for me?

I must not try to control Chris financially
I must be better at business + give
Natalie the £980 so she breaks even.
This will bring me more work + everyone
around her will have more respect
for me + clear the debt - It was Tw paid
not me.

Assimilate: How can I use the principles to achieve my goals/riches?

I will always do the right thing
+ never RIP ANYONE off especially
my friends or myself.

Apply: How am I going to use it? Action steps. Do It Now!

I am going to ask Natalie to invoice me
at next week when I get paid.

The Impression of Increase - One

1.   What are some of the actions that you are currently doing that convey the impression of increase to others?

- Dressing better, always wear make-up + jewellery before I leave the house.
- Always tell people how well I am doing
- Always give thanks publicly
- Be generous with gifts
- Never turn up empty-handed

2.   What other actions can you do that will convey the impression of increase. How will you do this? When will you do this?

I will be generous to myself by asking for my expenses to be paid, by tipping in resturants + by speaking nicely always to my husband even if I am irritated, I will always be kind + generous to myself, my husband + my family, colleagues, clients + friends, etc but especially to staff, NEVER BE A DIVA AGAIN Please help me God, Sri Amma Bhagavan + the Angels + Jesus Christ. XXX.

The Impression of Increase - Two

1.   What might you do to help two other people advance? List their names. Describe what you can do to help them advance. Specifically how and when will you do this?

Chris T-T - I can help by promoting + supporting his work + buying his T-shirts to sell

Deeksha group - helping them to receive from the Divine

Lorna, sue,

Helen
Stef - I can help by swapping treatments + support

The whole SheSays Brighton network - creating a supporting strong ~~net~~ connections

Veronica - helping her with her blog

Natalie + Krit - Get them a home they love in a location they love

Mum - Get her an ipad

Luis - Get him a dream job

Reiki people - help them fulfil their dreams as healers

Mike - help him be awakened

Lorna - help her find her dream job + a new lovely relationship

Online OM viewers - help everyone who watches become awakened

As a result of your new learnings list the actions or goals will you are going to accomplish, so that you too can become rich by doing things "in a certain way"

1. Find my dream home

2. Help others

3. Be nicer + less controlling + rude to Chris

4. Be nicer to strangers in cafés especially

5. Be better at asking the Divine for help

6. Be the best that I can Be

Chapter Fifteen - The Advancing Man

What I have said in the last chapter applies as well to the professional man and the wage-earner as to the man who is engaged in mercantile business.

No matter whether you are a physician, a teacher, or a clergyman, if you can give increase of life to others and make them sensible of the fact, they will be attracted to you, and you will get rich. The physician who holds the vision of himself as a great and successful healer, and who works toward the complete realization of that vision with faith and purpose, as described in former chapters, will come into such close touch with the Source of Life that he will be phenomenally successful; patients will come to him in throngs.

No one has a greater opportunity to carry into effect the teachings of this book than the practitioner of medicine; it does not matter to which of the various schools he may belong, for the principle of healing is common to all of them, and may be reached by all alike. The Advancing Man in medicine, who holds to a clear mental image of himself as successful, and who obeys the laws of faith, purpose, and gratitude, will cure every curable case he undertakes, no matter what remedies he may use.

In the field of religion, the world cries out for the clergyman who can teach his hearers the true science of abundant life. He who masters the details of the science of getting rich, together with the allied sciences of being well, of being great, and of winning love, and who teaches these details from the pulpit, will never lack for a congregation. This is the gospel that the world needs; it win give increase of life, and men will hear it gladly, and will give liberal support to the man who brings it to them.

What is now needed is a demonstration of the science of life from the pulpit. We want preachers who can not only tell us how, but who in their own persons will show us how. We need the preacher who will himself be rich, healthy, great, and beloved, to teach us how to attain to these things; and when he comes he will find a numerous and loyal following.

211

The same is true of the teacher who can inspire the children with the faith and purpose of the advancing life. He will never be "out of a job." And any teacher who has this faith and purpose can give it to his pupils; he cannot help giving it to them if it is part of his own life and practice.

What is true of the teacher, preacher, and physician is true of the lawyer, dentist, real estate man, insurance agent—of everybody.

The combined mental and personal action I have described is infallible; it cannot fail. Every man and woman who follows these instructions steadily, perseveringly, and to the letter, will get rich. The law of the Increase of Life is as mathematically certain in its operation as the law of gravitation; getting rich is an exact science.

The wage earner will find this as true of his case as of any of the others mentioned. Do not feel that you have no chance to get rich because you are working where there is no visible opportunity for advancement, where wages are small and the cost of living high. Form your clear mental vision of what you want, and begin to act with faith and purpose.

Do all the work you can do, every day, and do each piece of work in a perfectly successful manner; put the power of success, and the purpose to get rich, into everything that you do.

But do not do this merely with the idea of currying favor with your employer, in the hope that he, or those above you, will see your good work and advance you; it is not likely that they will do so.

The man who is merely a "good" workman, filling his place to the very best of his ability, and satisfied with that, is valuable to his employer; and, it is not to the employer's interest to promote he is worth more where he is.

To secure advancement, something more is necessary than to be too large for your place.

The man who is certain to advance is the one who is too big for his place, and who has a clear concept of what he wants to be; who knows that he can become what he wants to be, and who is determined to BE what he wants to be.

Do not try to more than fill your present place with a view to pleasing your employer; do it with the idea of advancing yourself. Hold the faith and purpose of increase during work hours, after work hours, and before work hours. Hold it in such a way that every person who comes in contact with you, whether foreman, fellow workman, or social acquaintance, will feel the power of purpose radiating from you; so that every one will get the sense of advancement and increase from you. Men will be attracted to you, and if there is no possibility for advancement in your present job, you will very soon see an opportunity to take another job.

There is a Power which never fails to present opportunity to the Advancing Man who is moving in obedience to law.

God cannot help helping you, if you act in a Certain Way; He must do so in order to help Himself.

There is nothing in your circumstances or in the industrial situation that can keep you down. If you cannot get rich working for a conglomerate, you can get rich on a ten-acre farm; and if you begin to move in the Certain Way, you will certainly escape from the "clutches" of the steel trust and get on to the farm or wherever else you wish to be.

If a few thousands of its employees would enter upon the Certain Way, the steel trust would soon be in a bad plight; it would have to give its workingmen more opportunity, or go out of business. Nobody has to work for a trust; the trust can keep men in so-called hopeless conditions only so long as there are men who are too ignorant to know of science of getting rich, or too intellectually slothful to practice it.

Begin this way of thinking and acting, and your faith and purpose will make you quick to see any opportunity to better your condition.

Such opportunities will speedily come, for the Supreme, working in All, and working for you, will bring them before you.

Do not wait for an opportunity to be all that you want to be; when an opportunity, to be more than you are now is presented and you feel impelled toward it, take it. It win be the first toward a greater opportunity.

There is no such thing possible in this universe as a lack of opportunities for the man who is living the advancing life.

It is inherent in the constitution of the cosmos that all things shall be for him and work together for his good, and he must certainly get rich if he acts and thinks in the Certain Way. So let wage-earning men and women study this book with great care, and enter with confidence upon the course of action it prescribes; it will not fail.

Chapter Fifteen - Taking Action
Understanding Chapter Fifteen
The Advancing Man

1. What impression should a professional person seek to give?

    To give the increase of life to others
    Radiate advancement
    BE greater than who you are

2. How must a worker who can see no visible chance for advancement do?

    Hold a clear vision for advancement
    in all your hours, feel the power
    of purpose radiating out from
    you to everyone. BE BEST.

3. What would happen to a company if many of its employees enter into the Science of Getting Rich?

    It would have to give its workers more
    opportunities or go out of business.

"Energy flows where attention goes."

"What you focus upon expands."

Extraordinary people are just ordinary people who have plans to do extraordinary things."

Chapter Fifteen Learnings

The most Important principles, concepts and thoughts that I have learned from this Chapter are:

1. _Every person in any profession can give the increase of life to others_

2. _This combined mental + personal action is infallible, it cannot fail_

3. _Every person who follows it, will get rich._

4. _Do all the work you can do in a perfectly successful manner_

5. _Put the power of purpose, success + the purpose to get rich + it will happen._

6. Don't do this way in order to be a good worker for your employer

7. BE TOO BIG FOR YOUR WORKPLACE

8. Hold the feeling of advancement with everyone you came into contact with, Radiate Success.

Chapter Fifteen Learnings

The two most Important principles, concepts and thoughts that I have learned from this Chapter and will use in my life are:

Principle One:

This Certain Way is unfalliable

_____

_____

_____

_____

Principle Two:

Be too big for your workplace

_____

_____

_____

_____

_____

"He who expands consciousness so as to measure things largely gains capacity, while he who takes a small view of everything remains incompetent. We do not get power, growth or ability by trying to cram a small mind, but by trying to expand the mind. And to expand the mind we must take the largest possible view of all things."
– Christian D. Larson

Putting the Science of Getting Rich Principles to Work

Recognize: Principle One I recognize in this Chapter is:

This way is unfallable

Relate: What does this mean to me? What will this principle do for me?

If I follow all the instructions, review +
keep holding a clear vision of what
I want, be grateful + radiate success
I will be ~~the~~ rich + have all the
things I want

Assimilate: How can I use the principles to achieve my goals/riches?

Remember to ~~be~~ keep refining and
adding to my goal + keep expanding
+ being the best I can be +
continuously expand.

Apply: How am I going to use it? Action steps. Do It Now!

Look for the house I want now
Know it is coming
Plan exactly how I will spend, save +
be rich every day.
How does it feel to be financially
independent + financially free!

Putting the Science of Getting Rich Principles to Work

Recognize: Principle Two I recognize in this Chapter is:

Be bigger

Relate: What does this mean to me? What will this principle do for me?

Be always the best, help others
to be the best they can be
continually radiate + expand
BE NICE

Assimilate: How can I use the principles to achieve my goals/riches?

Being nice
Be honest
Have inner integrity
Be grateful
Do all that I can do in the best way
possible each day

Apply: How am I going to use it? Action steps. Do It Now!

Just be nicer
Be better
Go where I am guided
Go where my passion is
Help when I can

The Advancing Man - One

My plan to be too big for my current position.

1.   What can you do to give increase of life to others, right now?

Help my reiki clients
Travel to do OM's, listen to others,
help them where I can
Be positive, be happy, be nice

2.   Choose one of the above and write down how and when you will give the "increase of life" that you have described above?

Tomorrow I will help Lewis by giving him
the laptop, supporting him in his work
+ by be radiating positive energy for
his work, now + the future

3.   "The man who is certain to advance is one who is too big for his place AND has a clear concepts of what he wants to be; who knows that he can become what he wants to be, and who is determined to BE what he wants to be."

   a) My clear concept of what I want to be is: A powerful mentor, trainer, broadcaster, writer, healer, guru + teacher

   b) I know I can become what I want to be because: I have created a powerful network of allies, around the world + I am a onemen Meditator.

The Advancing Man - Two

1. I am determined to be what I want to be. These are the reasons why; I am determined.

I am a Oneness Meditator
I have powerful allies
God the Creator is my best friend +
my benevolant father.
I just need to know what I want
+ it shall be given to me.
Money is needed to be the best that
I can be + ~~creat~~ creating riches
is my divine right.

2. The things that I can do right now to do more than fill my present position are:

I can always look + be good at everything
I do. I can always plan my money
help take things to India, pack the
right things + take honey to SviBhagavan.
know everything I do every day is
SUCCESSFUL if I do the best I can do.

As a result of your new learnings list the actions or goals will you are going to accomplish, so that you too can become rich by doing things "in a certain way"

1. _____

_____

_____

_____

2. _____

_____

_____

_____

3. _____

_____

_____

_____

4. _____

_____

_____

_____

5. _____

_____

_____

_____

6. _____

_____

_____

Chapter Sixteen - Some Cautions, And Concluding Observations

Many people will scoff at the idea that there is an exact science of getting rich; holding the impression that the supply of wealth is limited, they will insist that social and governmental institutions must be changed before even any considerable number of people can acquire a competence.

But this is not true.

It is true that some existing governments keep the masses in poverty, but this is because the masses do not think and act in the Certain Way.

If the masses begin to move forward as suggested in this book, neither governments nor industrial systems can check them; all systems must be modified to accommodate the forward movement.

If the people have the Advancing Mind, have the Faith that they can become rich, nothing can possibly keep them in poverty.

Individuals may enter upon the Certain Way at any time, and under any government, and make themselves rich, and when any considerable number of individuals do so under any government, they will cause the system to be so modified as to open the way for others.

The more men who get rich on the competitive plane, the worse for others; the more who get rich on the creative plane, the better for others.

The economic salvation of the masses can only be accomplished by getting a large number of people to practice the scientific method set down in, this book, and become rich. These will show others the way, and inspire them with a desire for real life, with the faith that it can be attained, and with the purpose to attain it.

For the present, however, it is enough to know that neither the government, under which you live nor the capitalistic or competitive system of industry can keep you from getting rich. When you enter upon the creative plane of thought you will rise above all these things and become a citizen of another kingdom.

But remember that your thought must be held upon the creative plane; you are never for an instant to be betrayed into regarding the supply as limited, or into acting on the moral level of competition.

Whenever you do fall into old ways of thought, correct yourself instantly; for when you are in the competitive mind, you have lost the co-operation of the Mind of the Whole.

Do not spend any time in planning as to how you will meet possible emergencies in the future, except as the necessary policies may affect your actions to-day. You are concerned with doing to-day's work in a perfectly successful manner, and not with emergencies which may arise to-morrow; you can attend to them as they come.

Do not concern yourself with questions as to how you shall surmount obstacles which may loom upon your business horizon, unless you can see plainly that your course must be altered today in order to avoid them.

No matter how tremendous an obstruction may appear at a distance, you will find that if you go on in the Certain Way it will disappear as you approach it, or that a way over, through, or around it will appear.

No possible combination of circumstances can defeat a man or woman who is proceeding to get rich along strictly scientific lines. No man or woman who obeys the law can fail to get rich, any more than one can multiply two by two and fail to get four.

Give no anxious thought to possible disasters, obstacles, panics, or unfavorable combinations of circumstances; it is time enough to meet such things when they present themselves before you in the immediate present, and you will find that every difficulty carries with it the wherewithal for its overcoming.

Guard your speech. Never speak of yourself, your affairs, or of anything else in a discouraged or discouraging way.

Never admit the possibility of failure, or speak in a way that infers failure as a possibility.

Never speak of the times as being hard, or of business conditions as being doubtful. Times may be hard and business doubtful for those who are on the competitive plane, but they can never be so for you; you can create what you want, and you are above fear.

When others are having hard times and poor business, you will find your greatest opportunities.

Train yourself to think of and to look upon the world as a something which is Becoming, which is growing; and to regard seeming evil as being only that which is undeveloped. Always speak in terms of advancement; to do otherwise is to deny your faith, and to deny your faith is to lose it.

Never allow yourself to feel disappointed. You may expect to have a certain thing at a certain time, and not get it at that time; and this will appear to you like failure.

But if you hold to your faith you will find that the failure is only apparent.

Go on in the certain way, and if you do not receive that thing, you will receive something so much better that you will see that the seeming failure was really a great success.

A student of this science had set his mind on making a certain business combination which seemed to him at the time to be very desirable, and he worked for some weeks to bring it about. When the crucial time came, the thing failed in a perfectly inexplicable way; it was as if some unseen influence had been working secretly against him. He was not disappointed; on the contrary, he thanked God that his desire had been overruled, and went steadily on with a grateful mind. In a few weeks an opportunity so much better came his way that he would not have made the first deal on any account; and he saw that a Mind which knew more than he knew had prevented him from losing the greater good by entangling himself with the lesser.

That is the way every seeming failure will work out for you, if you keep your faith, hold to your purpose, have gratitude, and do, every day, all that can be done that day, doing each separate act in a successful manner.

When you make a failure, it is because you have not asked enough; keep on, and a larger thing than you were seeking will certainly come to you. Remember this.

You will not fail because you lack the necessary talent to do what you wish to do. If you go on as I have directed, you will develop all the talent that is necessary to the doing of your work.

It is not within the scope of this book to deal with the science of cultivating talent; but it is as certain and simple as the process of getting rich.

However, do not hesitate or waver for fear that when you come to any certain place you will fail for lack of ability; keep right on, and when you come to that place, the ability will be furnished to you. The same source of Ability which enabled the untaught Lincoln to do the greatest work in government ever accomplished by a single man is open to you; you may draw upon all the mind there is for wisdom to use in meeting the responsibilities which are laid upon you. Go on in full faith.

Study this book. Make it your constant companion until you have mastered all the ideas contained in it. While you are getting firmly established in this faith, you will do well to give up most recreations and pleasures, and to stay away from places where ideas conflicting with these are advanced in lectures or sermons. Do not read pessimistic or conflicting literature, or get into arguments upon the matter. Do very little reading outside of the writers mentioned in the Preface. Spend most of your leisure time in contemplating your vision, and in cultivating gratitude, and in reading this book. It contains all you need to know of the science of getting rich; and you will find all the essentials summed up in the following chapter.

Chapter Sixteen - Taking Action
Understanding Chapter Sixteen
Some Cautions and Concluding Observations

1. What would happen if the masses began to move forward as outlined in the Science of Getting Rich?

    All systems would have to be modified to accommodate - like The Internet Industry

2. How should you cope with future emergencies and obstacles?

    Deal with them as they arise not worrying now about unforeseen problems.

3. Describe how to guard your speech?

    Never speak of ~~yourself~~ myself or my business affairs or anything else in a discouraging manner.

4. What must you do if you expect something or something to happen and it does not? Is this failure? Explain.

    Be grateful that God has protected you + to ask for something even better + it will appear. This is never failure.

"Without doubt the most common weakness of all human beings is the habit of leaving their own mind open to the negative influence of other people and their own negative thoughts and speech."

Chapter Sixteen Learnings

The most Important principles, concepts and thoughts that I have learned from this Chapter are:

1. This way is for everyone, If we all used it to the current systems would change to accomodate it.

2. If I work on the creative plane everyone benefits

3. It doesn't matter which government or which system is governing me I can get rich.

4. I can mustn't spend too time planning for emergencies in the future

5. GUARD MY SPEECH. Only speak in terms of success about myself + my business

6. _Never admit the possibility of failure_

7. _If I don't get something I want, I know_
something even bigger + better is coming

8. _I have FAITH in this way, + in God_
+ the expanding universe.

Chapter Sixteen Learnings

The two most Important principles, concepts and thoughts that I have learned from this Chapter and will use in my life are:

Principle One:

Never admit the possibility of failure
Guard your speech
Avoid negative people

Principle Two:

Do not spend time on worrying
about future disasters or depressions
Have faith only good things are coming.

"We need to be careful of what we think and talk about because thoughts run in currents as real as those of air and water. Of what we think and talk about we attract to us a like current of thought. This acts on our mind and body for good or for ill." – Prentice Mulford.

"No man and no institution was ever ridden down or talked down by anything but itself." – Emerson

Putting the Science of Getting Rich Principles to Work

Recognize: Principle One I recognize in this Chapter is:

Guard Your thoughts

Relate: What does this mean to me? What will this principle do for me?

Be VERY CAREFUL not to judge myself, Chris + others. Be positive + always speak of myself in terms of success.

Assimilate: How can I use the principles to achieve my goals/riches?

By knowing I am always successful each + every day, I do not entertain any thoughts of negativity, I cannot fail to be rich.

Apply: How am I going to use it? Action steps. Do It Now!

STOP MOANING ABOUT MYSELF + OTHERS
BE POSITIVE. NEVER EVER PUT MYSELF DOWN
NEVER BE SELF-DEPRICATING
KNOW THAT BY BEING RICH + SUCCESSFUL
THIS IS GOD'S FULL EXPRESSION WORKING
THROUGH ME.

Putting the Science of Getting Rich Principles to Work

Recognize: Principle Two I recognize in this Chapter is:

Stop worrying about the future

Relate: What does this mean to me? What will this principle do for me?

There is always work, projects, contacts
There is an abundance
There is no need to scrabble for work or
for property or anything

Assimilate: How can I use the principles to achieve my goals/riches?

Know that there is plenty for everyone
Know that my priorities are not the same
as others + that I can make my own
mind up about saving for the future or
~~front~~

Apply: How am I going to use it? Action steps. Do It Now!

Keep doing my homework
TRUST IN GOD that I will always be provided for
LOVE THE PROCESS

Guarding Your Speech

"When amongst many, guard you speech and when alone, guard your thoughts."

Buddhist Saying

"Watch your thoughts; they become your words. Watch your words; they become your actions. Watch your actions; they become your habits. Watch your habits; they become your character. Watch your character for it will become your destiny. If I am not for myself; who will be for me? If I am only for myself; what am I? And if not now, when?"

Hillel

Guarding Your Speech One Day at a Time

Do you think that you can go for twenty-four hours without saying anything negative or unkind about or to anyone? Commit to this life changing exercise. Resolve that you will not say anything negative about another person or yourself. Throughout the day, as you interact with others, constantly monitor what you say and make every effort to guard your speech. Record your thoughts, results and feelings below.

_____

_____

_____

_____

_____

_____

My Commitment

Study this book. Make it your constant companion until you have mastered all the ideas contained in it. While you are getting firmly established in this faith, you will do well to give up most recreations and pleasures; and to stay away from places where ideas conflicting with these are advanced in lectures or sermons. Do not read pessimistic or conflicting literature, or get into arguments upon the matter. Do very little reading outside of the writers mentioned in the Preface. Spend most of your leisure time in contemplating your vision, and in cultivating gratitude, and in reading this book.

Write out a commitment that you will continue the study of the Science of Getting Rich until all that you want you have.

My Commitment is _to continue to read + re-read this book + embody all the principles + check my thoughts, + keep a clear vision + do not discuss or argue about it, keep my own leisure time to growing + learning + advancing + every day to be successful + never dwell on the failure — past or future._

R Thorpe-Tracey
Signature

1 Nov 2013.
Date

As a result of your new learnings list the actions or goals will you are going to accomplish, so that you too can become rich by doing things "in a certain way"

1. Be grateful

2. Give thanks

3. Be positive

4. Keep checking in

5. Keep my own counsel

6. Ask for help from the Divine.

Chapter Seventeen - Summary Of Science Of Getting Rich

There is a thinking stuff from which all things are made, and which, in its original state, permeates, penetrates, and fills the interspaces of the universe.

A thought in this substance produces the thing that is imagined by the thought.

Man can form things in his thought, and by impressing his thought upon formless substance can cause the thing he think about to be created.

In order to do this, man must pass from the competitive to the creative mind; otherwise he cannot be in harmony with the Formless Intelligence, which is always creative and never competitive in spirit.

Man may come into full harmony with the Formless Substance by entertaining a lively and sincere gratitude for the blessings it bestows upon him. Gratitude unifies the mind of man with the intelligence of Substance, so that man's thoughts are received by the Formless. Man can remain upon the creative plane only by uniting himself with the Formless Intelligence through a deep and continuous feeling of gratitude.

Man must form a clear and definite mental image of the things he wishes to have, to do, or to become; and he must hold this mental image in his thoughts, while being deeply grateful to the Supreme that all his desires are granted to him. The man who wishes to get rich must spend his leisure hours in contemplating his Vision, and in earnest thanksgiving that the reality is being given to him. Too much stress cannot be laid on the importance of frequent contemplation of the mental image, coupled with unwavering faith and devout gratitude. This is the process by which the impression is given to the Formless, and the creative forces set in motion.

The creative energy works through the established channels of natural growth, and of the industrial and social order. All that is included in his mental image will surely be brought to the man who follows the instructions given above, and whose faith does not waver. What he wants will come to him through the ways of established trade and commerce.

In order to receive his own when it shall come to him, man must be active; and this activity can only consist in more than filling his present place. He must keep in mind the Purpose to get rich through the realization of his mental image. And he must do, every day, all that can be done that day, taking care to do each act in a successful manner. He must give to every man a use value in excess of the cash value he receives, so that each transaction makes for more life, and he must so hold the Advancing Thought that the impression of Increase will be communicated to all with whom he comes in contact.

The men and women who practice the foregoing instructions will certainly get rich, and the riches they receive will be in exact proportion to the definiteness of their vision, the fixity of their purpose, the steadiness of their faith, and the depth of their gratitude.

Final Actions:

1.   Read the Summary of The Science of Getting Rich over and over again until you have internalized it.

2.   Read The Science of Getting Rich until it becomes part of your life.

3.   As a result of your new learnings **list the top 10 actions or goals** will you are going to accomplish, so that you too can become rich by doing things "in a certain way"? Summarize the top 10 actions or goals that you listed at the end of each chapter below. As a result of your new learnings list the actions or goals will you are going to accomplish, so that you too can become rich by doing things "in a certain way"

① Do OMS every week online

② Organise OMS around the country + Europe

③ Be grateful + give thanks every day

④ Finish Do the wish book for all areas

⑤ Visualize the house clearly

⑥ Visualize the business

⑦ Visualize the income I get £250,000 → £1m per annum

⑧ Start writing my books

⑨ Get my radio show

⑩ Be the best that I can be every day.

_____

_____

_____

_____

_____

_____

_____

_____

_____

_____

Proven, Time-Tested Secrets And Materials That Work
To Produce Health, Wealth And Happiness

www.ProsperitySecrets.com and www.WallaceWattles.com publish practical, life-changing books, e-books, self-study courses, e-classes, CDs and audiocassettes, and videos to assist clients and customers in living their lives more completely.

We are dedicated to provide you with proven, effective, time-tested secrets and materials that work to produce health, wealth and happiness.

A partial list of some of our customers' favorite ebooks are:

The Science of Getting Rich

The Science of Getting Rich Action Pack

The Science of Being Great

The Master Key

The Ideal Made Real

Thinking For Results

Mastery of Self

Mastery of Fate

How to Stay Young

The Hidden Secret

Prosperity Through Thought Forces

Visit www.ProsperitySecrets.com, www.WallaceWattles.com or any of our other associated websites to obtain these marvelous books and get information on the many other books published by ProsperitySecrets.com Inc.

About the Authors

Larry McLauchlin is a specialist in communication, and individual and corporate transformations. He has spent the over 30 years researching and making practical the structure of communication, persuasion, influence, financial literacy, leadership and spirituality.

Larry's major project is to bring the wisdom of early 1900s authors, such as, Christian Larson, Wallace Wattles, Charles F. Haanel and others to the general public. Larry currently has published over 30 spiritual, inspirational, self-help e-books through www.ProsperitySecrets.com and www.Spiritual-e-books.com.

He is a Certified Master Practitioner of Neuro-Linguistic Programming. And has spent thousands of hour compiling, understanding, internalizing and training in advanced language patterns, hypnosis and how the mind works. He is the internationally known author of Advanced Language Patterns Mastery.

For a catalog of his books and tapes, to read dozens of free articles by him or to sign up for his free newsletters visit Larry's main websites at: www.ProsperitySecrets.com, www.nlpandhypnosis.com, and www.Spiritual-e-books.com or email him at larry@ProsperitySecrets.com.

Wallace Wattles (1860-1911) While it is difficult to discover much about Wallace Delois Wattles' life, it is known that he was born in the United States. And that he initially lived a life consisting of failure, defeat and poverty. But then latter in his life, after studying, practicing and applying the principles that he writes about in his books he turn his life completely around.

Printed in the United States
41343LVS00005B/127-130